MEYER LANSKY

MEYER LANSKY

The Shadowy Exploits of New York's Master Manipulator

GANGSTER

by Art Montague

PUBLISHED BY ALTITUDE PUBLISHING LTD.
1500 Railway Avenue, Canmore, Alberta T1W 1P6
www.altitudepublishing.com
1-800-957-6888

Extreme care has been taken to ensure that all information presented in
this book is accurate and up to date. Neither the author nor the
publisher can be held responsible for any errors.

Publisher	Stephen Hutchings
Associate Publisher	Kara Turner
Series Editor	Jill Foran
Editor	Lori Burwash
Digital Photo Colouring	Bryan Pezzi

We acknowledge the financial support of the Government
of Canada through the Book Publishing Industry Development
Program (BPIDP) for our publishing activities.

Altitude GreenTree Program
Altitude Publishing will plant twice as many trees as were used
in the manufacturing of this product.

Cataloging in Publication Data

Montague, Art
Meyer Lansky / Art Montague.

(Amazing stories)
ISBN 1-55265-100-2

1. Lansky, Meyer, 1902- 2. Lansky, Meyer, 1902-1983. 3.
Criminals--
United States--Biography. 4. Organized crime--United States--History--20th
century. I. Title. II. Series: Amazing stories (Canmore, Alta.)

HV6248.L36M65 2005   364.1'092   C2005-901371-0

An application for the trademark for Amazing Stories™
has been made and the registered trademark is pending.

Printed and bound in Canada by Friesens
2 4 6 8 9 7 5 3 1

The history of organized crime in New York City has long been glamorized through
books, magazines, film, and television. Inevitably, anyone researching this history
will be presented with many different "true accounts" of underworld events. In
regards to each title in the Amazing Stories series, Altitude Publishing has left it
up to the author to choose which version of events he or she wishes to convey.

To jazz musician Jill McCarron,
whose adopted home, New York City,
continues to be a place of dreams
and source of inspiration.

Contents

Prologue

It was January 1914, and New York City's winter was harsher than usual. On this particular January afternoon, as gray and frigid as the water of the East River, a small, sullen boy named Meyer Lansky was hurrying down Hester Street, hunched against the wind's bite. Home was a block away.

Suddenly, he stopped in his tracks. He was surrounded, walled in by a gang of Sicilian teenagers. If he had been paying attention, he could have crossed the street to avoid them. Now it was too late.

Meyer recognized the gang. Most Jewish kids in the neighborhood knew them, paying them a nickel a week in protection money. The alternative was repeated beatings. The gang's leader, Salvatore Lucania, was five years older than Meyer, stood a head taller, and had a reputation as a bully who was brutally quick with his fists.

Any cry for help from Meyer would be wasted on pass-ersby — on East Side streets, people did what they could to avoid confrontations. Non-involvement was the norm. Meyer was on his own, and Salvatore was in his face, demanding the nickel tribute.

"There was nothing to him," Salvatore later recalled. "He was a short skinny kid, a matchstick I could have snapped in

a second. Any of us could have."

But Meyer wasn't about to go down without a fight. He pulled his hands from his pockets, his fists already clenched. Tensely, he lifted his head, looked the threatening Sicilian directly in the eye, and retorted, "Go #&@! yourself."

Later, Salvatore said he admired the "gutsy punk." Meyer's surprising, almost laughable bravado saved him from a certain beating. Salvatore relented — this fish was too small to be anything but a throwback. He defused the situation and, to save face with his gang, threw an ominous parting warning to Meyer as he trudged up Hester with his entourage: "We'll be back."

Indeed, the two were destined to meet again, but never once would they raise a hand against each other. Meyer would become known as "the Little Man," Salvatore as "Lucky Luciano." Working together, the pair would go on to shape the foundation and face of organized crime in America.

Chapter 1
Welcome to America

hen out on the street, Meyer Lansky learned that to keep his head down and keep walking usually meant safe passage. The practice generally served him well during his first years in New York City, but he had learned it in Poland years before.

According to information provided by his father to U.S. immigration authorities, Meyer was born Meyer Suchowljansky in Grodno, Poland, on July 4, 1902. Unlike the Jews in much of eastern Europe, up until the last decade of the 19th century, those living in Grodno had escaped the fury of anti-Semitic pogroms. These massacres routinely left Jewish homes and shops looted and burned, and people injured, killed, or kidnapped for army service. By the turn of the century, however, the Russian tsar, who then controlled that part of Poland, legalized persecution of the Jews, and his bureaucrats incited pogroms against them. Grodno became a center for armed Jewish resistance.

Meyer and his family — his parents, younger brother Jacob (Jake), and grandparents — endured. The worst times, Meyer recounted, were during Easter and Passover, when roaming bands of Christian peasants would riot throughout the Jewish sector with the active support of police officials. Meyer recalled his family burying their valuables in their backyard in advance of these marauders. He also recalled a young Jewish soldier urging his parents and grandparents to fight violence with violence. Meyer then saw the same soldier in the streets recruiting other young men and, in the woods, training his recruits in the use of contraband firearms.

The Suchowljansky family was well respected in Grodno. Yet, at the family dinner table young Meyer heard his father and grandfather discuss an incident in which his uncle had had his arm severed by a Russian Cossack with one sweep of a saber, without provocation. He witnessed his parents and grandparents abused in the streets by Gentile toughs and peasants. He witnessed Jews submissively turning the other cheek, only to have that slapped or spat upon, too. Respect within Grodno's close-knit Jewish community was no safeguard in relations with non-Jews.

Worse than the pogroms for Meyer and the other Jews of Grodno was the fear — the fear of knowing worse was to come, knowing worse was inevitable, but not knowing when.

The fear hung over Grodno's Jewish population, infecting every hour. From it emerged three choices for Jews: stay and suffer; emigrate to Palestine, the Jewish Holy Land; or emigrate to America and embrace the promising future that life there seemed to offer, so they were told.

Meyer's grandfather, Benjamin Suchowljansky, was no firebrand. Nor was he a fool. "Enough," the old man proclaimed one day. "We must leave or be destroyed."

Grandfather Benjamin chose Jerusalem. During family councils he argued that America — if not now, then later — would be as anti-Semitic as anywhere Jews and Gentiles tried to co-exist. But Meyer's father, Max, did not share Benjamin's desire to settle in the Holy Land. He wanted a place where his family could grow and prosper, and he believed America offered more opportunity.

In 1909, Max traveled alone to New York City to work, save money, and eventually bring his wife and two sons out of Poland. During the two years that passed before the family was reunited, Meyer began to see himself as his mother's man of the house. As was her wish, he devoted more time to religious studies. In their home he was always willing to take on extra tasks, run errands, and, most important, serve as Jake's male authority figure. He became Jake's teacher, protector, confidant, and sometime disciplinarian.

This feeling of responsibility intensified in 1910, when Grandfather Benjamin, with his wife Basha, moved to Jerusalem. Benjamin died later that year, followed in a month by his wife. With his grandfather's passing, Meyer lost more than a friend; he lost his own mentor. For countless hours the old man had held him rapt describing Jewish history — not just stories of persecutions and adversity, but also the special times of celebration, perseverance, and victory. Through his grandfather's teachings, Meyer had learned the importance of the family unit, its inherent strength, and the ways in which it extended into the community outside the home.

Meyer's grandfather was more than a talker. His life in Grodno was an example of his words. Benjamin had been a respected middle-class businessman, recognized for his devotion to Judaism and to his family, his first concerns. His generosity had been so well known and so extensive in the community that, when he emigrated to Jerusalem, he barely had enough money to pay the fares. Meyer characterized him as a man so rich in life, understanding, and faith that he had no need of a fat bank account. The reality, however, was that Benjamin was forced to abandon his house and business when he left because the laws of the day prevented him, as a Jew, from selling them. Yet Benjamin's way of life in Grodno continued to have an impact on his grandson, even after his death. When old himself, Meyer once said, "Even now I sometimes wake up in the night feeling the warmth of his personality surrounding me."

Throughout 1910, Meyer and his family in Grodno lived on savings. For the first time in his life, Meyer was feeling the pinch of poverty. Neighbors rallied to help, but their assistance was meager. Jews, who had once made up 70 percent of Grodno's 40,000 people, were leaving in droves for Israel and America. Many families in the same straits as Meyer's were also waiting for money from America for their own exodus.

By 1911, Meyer's father had saved enough money to bring his family out of the threatening eastern European borderlands and establish them in New York City. The family traveled by train from Grodno to the port of Odessa — for Meyer and Jake, a journey bubbling with excitement. But in Odessa, a crooked shipping agent bilked Meyer's mother out of their boat fares. Desolated, and almost penniless, she sold the last of the family jewelry and borrowed from other New York–bound Grodno Jews, finally making up enough for their passage across the Atlantic. They traveled on a rusted, overcrowded tramp steamer that threatened to founder every time a wave splashed against it. Meyer recalled being seasick for most of the journey, but he hid this from his mother by sneaking outside to be sick over the rail. He preferred putting on a brave front to being an added worry.

Seasickness was forgotten as the old freighter churned into New York, up through the Narrows and into the Hudson River, Brooklyn on one side, Staten Island on the other. The ship slowly passed between Governors and Liberty islands, the symbolic Statue of Liberty clearly visible from the deck, crowded with steerage passengers anxious for the first heartening glimpse of their future. They disembarked at Ellis Island — it was their first step, but they were within sight of the lower tip of Manhattan, Battery Park, and, just beyond, such streets of dreams as Broadway and Wall.

Cleared through Ellis Island, the family settled for a time in Brownsville, where Max rented a tenement flat in a predominantly Jewish neighborhood. The lifestyle lacked the security in which Meyer had grown up in his grandfather's house. Max was working long, hard hours as a garment presser just to pay the rent and keep food on the table. Day by day, Meyer watched his father's dream of a golden future seep into the dead-end drudgery of New York's garment district sweatshops. Hard times became harder. Eventually, after several moves within Brownsville, the family moved across the East River to the Lower East Side of Manhattan.

In 1912, the Lower East Side pulsated with action and opportunity, good and bad. "Getting ahead" energized the streets, even as poverty filled the tenements, crammed cheek to jowl, along them. Yiddish, flavored with the regional accents of polyglot eastern Europe, was the primary language of commerce on these streets. Added to the mix was some Italian and an occasional lilt of Irish accents. Of course, American English was also heard, partly because it was the language of many people's adopted country. However, English was also the language of crime on the Lower East Side, at least when different ethnic groups were communicating instead of preying on each other.

On the sidewalks, in the alleys, and sometimes blocking storefronts, legitimate and illegitimate commerce jockeyed for shelf space. Inside the buildings were saloons for hatching plots and cutting deals, stuss parlors for serious gamblers, and cigar stores taking bets from the more casual gamblers. Then there were the "dancing academies," which had more to do with prostitution than with twirling a partner across a dance floor.

Weather permitting, prostitutes openly plied their trade from the front stoops of their "shops," and every block had sidewalk crap games — fast, noisy, and crooked. Side by side with these were butchers and bakers, delis, clothiers, jewelers, furniture shops, horse stables, and, becoming more frequent, motorcar showrooms. Pushcart vendors and hawkers bawled their wares into the same din as the pimps and shills, the housewives haggling prices and freshness, the righteous yentas shrilly feeding the street's rumor mills from fire escapes as they hung out wet wash, and children yelling raucously as they ran errands, played, or committed some mischief.

For Meyer's father, the move to the Lower East Side was more than a step down the economic ladder — it was a fall off. Still, as best he could, he concentrated on preparing his sons for a better life. Their religion and many old Grodno customs remained central to the Lansky home.

Gone from Meyer's life, however, was the Jewish community life to which he had been accustomed in Grodno. Diminished was the importance of heder, the small instruction classes that emphasize diligent religious study and

Jewish history, taught with a view that the brightest sons would ultimately become rabbis. In its place were public schools, where hundreds of Jewish, Italian, and Irish immigrant children were lockstepped through a curriculum that gave little attention to ethnic differences, and less to ethnic history or religion.

Meyer had started public school in Brownsville at PS 84. Education was free in New York, and his father intended his sons to take advantage of it. Moreover, to help facilitate an easier transition to life in America, Meyer's father registered the two boys as "Lansky" rather than the more ponderous surname Suchowljansky.

Meyer's stint at PS 84 shaped his fascination with mathematics. He was exposed to what later became standard in Brooklyn public schools and other schools through New York's boroughs: the Baldane System of Primary Arithmetic. Although the system was in its infancy when Meyer attended PS 84, Saul Baldane was the school's principal. His system made arithmetic exciting and accessible to youngsters. It had relevance to them, perhaps even some magic. Certainly, it caught Meyer's mind and held it for life. Arithmetic became his passion, and Meyer's move to the Lower East Side did not abate it. Unfortunately, it found a juvenile expression at a sidewalk crap game.

Not yet in his teens, Meyer was a straight-A student at the East Side's PS 34 and a cocky arithmetic whiz who'd already decided he was about as streetwise as any other kid on the block. Still, he was closer to his family than to the street, and he took his family obligations seriously. On this occasion, New World ambition and precocious intelligence tested itself against Old World tradition.

Meyer's foremost duty for his family was delivery of the *cholent*, a succulent stew prepared days ahead for the Sabbath midday meal. The *cholent* was always delivered to the bakeshop on Delancey Street on Friday afternoon after school. It required slow baking in an oven, which most people in the tenements lacked. For a nickel apiece, a baker on Delancey rented space in his ovens to poor neighborhood Jewish families and carried out the final 12 hours of baking. For Meyer, delivering the family's *cholent* to the baker and then picking it up the next day was a considerable responsibility, a significant point of pride.

The route from Meyer's home on Grand Avenue to the bakery passed several sidewalk crap games on Delancey Street, games hard to miss despite the bustling congestion on the East Side's main drag. Even harder to miss was the fact that numbers were involved in those games. Odds and probability were likely alien concepts to young Meyer at the time, but he watched and calculated. Eventually he decided he could predict the winning rolls. Delivering the *cholent* for baking each week began to take a little longer — so did bringing it home. Meyer was captivated by the crap games — he was sure he'd found a way to make easy money.

Finally, one Friday afternoon, Meyer set the *cholent* on

the sidewalk, stepped up, and placed his first bet — the nickel meant to pay for the *cholent*. He lost. The nickel had been the family's last. In the Lansky home, there was no baked *cholent* that Sabbath.

Chastened, the youth vowed never again to let his family down. He also vowed never again to let chance weigh against him when he gambled. The streets had provided Meyer a lesson that school had not addressed.

Soon after his family moved to the Lower East Side, Meyer discovered the local libraries, the Seward Public Library and the Educational Alliance. Both filled their stacks with books aimed at the East Side's predominant population, first- and second-generation Jews from eastern Europe.

For Meyer, the libraries may have been refuges from his cramped tenement home and the area's chaotic, sometimes dangerous, streets. They were warm in winter, cool in summer — the opposite to what he had at home, on the streets, or even in school. Comfortably settled in, he would read with indiscriminate voracity. Soon he could as quickly quote Shakespeare as describe the latest progress in the Great War or the official doings of New York's city council. He was determined to get ahead; he just wasn't sure where that drive would take him.

Jake, the younger Lansky brother, worked hard, too, but learning did not come as easily for him. He relied on his older brother, and Meyer accepted that responsibility. It was a duty so ingrained that he may never have given it a thought.

Meyer's teachers remembered him as introverted and remarkably studious. In three years, he moved from grade one to six. However, he left school just shy of his 15th birthday, having graduated from grade eight. By then, the Lansky family had grown by three sisters, two of whom died. Financial pressure was overwhelming the family. In his father's view, Meyer was now old enough to begin contributing financially.

The work world for most youths on the Lower East Side consisted of a job in the rag trade. The garment industry was the area's principal employer — thankless, hopeless, and exploitative. Max knew that, but it was the only work he'd been able to obtain in America.

Max had seen the smoke rise from the Triangle Shirtwaist Company fire on March 25, 1911 — 146 employees died because exit doors were locked and fire ladders couldn't reach high enough to save them. He knew about the panic-stricken seamstresses, some only 14 years old, leaping from the building and smashing onto the sidewalks below.

But fire was the least of the hazards in the garment district. Mostly there was the slow and grinding sapping of energy brought on by too many hours, too many dim lights, impossible productivity demands, and fumes and fibers seeping into lungs, stomachs, and pores. And of course, employees were never paid enough money to compensate.

In the aftermath of the Triangle fire, Max witnessed the "improvements" of their conditions, when safety standards were instituted by politicians. He also knew which of these standards the appointed inspectors were bribed to ignore. He experienced the fledgling unions meant to protect his rights, but that instead charged him a fee to work (and the employer a fee to make sure there were no problems on the job). Max was a fundamentally honest man trying to make his way in a dishonest business. He wanted better for his eldest son. "I'll never let you do that," he told Meyer.

Instead, Max found his son a job as an apprentice machinist in a tool and die shop. He earned 10 cents an hour, 52 hours a week, but Meyer proved to be a quick study and enjoyed his work. His boss, delighted with his new employee's acumen, skill, and punctuality, foresaw Meyer making a dollar an hour within 20 years.

Meyer, however, was unimpressed. The work was fine, but he saw a different future for himself. Still convinced he could get rich by gambling, he continued to hang around the Delancey Street crap games. Indeed, he had made as much money gambling by the time he left school as he did in his new job.

It turned out that Meyer hadn't needed his arithmetic skills to win at craps. All he'd needed was the simple power of observation. It didn't take him long to figure out that the games were rigged. He saw the way loaded dice were introduced into a game at the last second to ensure a shill would win, and he'd bet with the shill. The men running the game knew what he was doing, but there were enough games that

Meyer could keep moving, never winning too much at one. As long as he did that, he was safe. Eventually his face became so familiar to the operators, they would occasionally hire him as a lookout or even a shill. Meyer began to feel that gambling might be his true calling, and the streets his natural habitat.

Chapter 2
Brains and Brawn

As a child, Meyer had witnessed sporadic violence on the streets of Grodno. However, on the streets of the Lower East Side during the first two decades of the 20th century, violence was an everyday occurrence: barroom brawls spilling onto the streets, pimps beating prostitutes, policemen cracking heads and rupturing spleens with their nightsticks, and wiseguys breaking up their competition's crap games (sometimes with guns).

Meyer's daily exposure to this violence had reconciled — if not inured — him to it. He came to see violence as a business option of last resort, a way of resolving business disputes in which the first to act or the last man standing, often the same person, was the apparent winner. Sometimes, however, the violence on the street struck closer to home and wasn't just business.

One day, he was quietly observing a crap game from a distance. This game was being operated by new people in the neighborhood, a surprise to Meyer because turf was controlled. Suddenly, a fight broke out and knives flashed. An eviction was under way — or was it? More hard men swarmed into the melee on the side of the newcomers. Guns came out and men began to fall, some shot, some stabbed or slashed, others hammered down with weighted pipes.

Meyer hid behind a fruit stand. This wasn't his fight. He had no stake in the outcome. Then, a tall dark-haired youth sprang into the brawl, scrambling for a gun lying in the street. He picked up the gun an instant before a thug with the same notion. The boy leveled the gun at the thug, obviously intending to shoot him. Police were already in sight.

Meyer had seen enough. He'd recognized the boy as Bennie Siegel, the son of a friend of his mother's. Leaping from his hideout, Meyer grabbed Bennie's arm, shouting, "You're crazy! Drop the gun and run!" For whatever reason, Bennie immediately did so, and the boys escaped the scene.

As soon as they were safely away, Bennie turned on Meyer. "Why didn't you let me kill the bastard? I needed the gun."

Young Meyer was unperturbed. "The police were right on the scene. If you'd been caught with the gun, you'd be in deep trouble. Only an idiot would shoot with the cops in sight. Use your head." Bennie reluctantly accepted the logic.

After that encounter, the two boys became close friends. For their own reasons, their mothers encouraged the relationship. Meyer's mother felt he was too much of a loner, a shy boy who avoided friendships. To her delight, it seemed that he was opening up, making friends, and becoming more a part of the Jewish community. Bennie's mother, meanwhile, felt that her "problem boy" had found a friend who would keep him out of trouble and set a good example.

Before he was out of his teen years, Bennie Siegel would become known as "Bugsy." He would become Meyer's trusted number two man — Meyer's go-to guy when persuasion and push failed and came to shove. Even Meyer conceded Bugsy was "crazy as a bedbug," hence the moniker, which was never used to his face without violent consequences. Meyer was the only man who could keep a leash on him, and sometimes Bennie would still manage to slip it.

Bennie was fearless and impulsive, the first person into a fray and the last person leaving it — quite unlike Meyer, who preferred to sidestep any fight he couldn't win. For his part, Bennie admired Meyer's toughness, which he found remarkable for someone so small, and the smoothness with which Meyer successfully navigated the East Side streets.

During those years, choosing sides was a prerequisite to survival on the streets, especially among small-time delinquents. Jews stuck with Jews, Italians with Italians, and Irish with Irish. The Irish had got there first and had no compunction about terrorizing the newcomers. The Italians wreaked their frustration on the Jews. But Meyer had learned a few lessons in Grodno. He was having none of it.

Meyer was thin, barely five-feet five, and not much to look at, but he could organize. Italian youth, he'd observed, had formed street gangs to fight off the Irish. He decided Jewish youth should do the same. His first recruit was the more-than-willing Bugsy Siegel. Then came his brother, Jake, who was much bigger than Meyer. Joseph "Doc" Stacher was another member. Doc was described by a biographer as the typical neighborhood "fat kid" and an inveterate crap player. However, when Doc tried to enlist for the Great War, he was rejected because he was too skinny, or so he said.

Meyer and Doc were drawn together by their love of gambling. Doc was always working on new systems to beat the odds. Sometimes Meyer would help him with the arithmetic, but mostly he counseled Doc on the futility of wagering. At the time, the message may have been lost because Meyer was a gambler himself.

There were others in Meyer's circle of buddies: Abner "Longie" Zwillman and his brother, Irving, Arthur Flegenheimer (later known as "Dutch Schultz"), and Louis "Lepke" Buchalter. Most of the crew had grown up together — same schools, same corners, same poverty, all Jews. And most remained loyal to Meyer throughout their lives.

Even as teenagers, the crew was showing signs that full-blown criminal careers were in the offing. Longie and Irving were adept pickpockets and purse-snatchers. If, as some-times happened, they slipped up, they could run like the wind. Their speed was also an asset when they committed smash-and-grab raids on merchants. Dutch Schultz made his pocket money rolling drunks, using the Good Samaritan guise of helping them make their way home. Lepke was a fix-ture in the garment district, stealing from wagons and trucks or right off the clothes racks as they were pushed along the street. There was nothing sneaky about his thieving — he was direct and vicious, unnecessarily beating up vendors before he robbed them.

Bugsy always liked to be around if there was the pros-pect of some rough stuff, but when it came to making money, he was proving himself to be quite a ladies' man. Tall and handsome, Bugsy spent most of his money on buying flashy clothes and squiring his girlfriends about the neighborhood. Bugsy wasn't a pimp. Instead, he provided prostitutes "pro-tection" services from both dissatisfied customers and overly greedy pimps.

Perhaps Bugsy's services appealed to Meyer's sense of chivalry. Meyer didn't like prostitution because he thought the women were vulnerable to exploitation, beatings, and even murder. But he was impressed enough with Bugsy's success that he decided to offer protection services him-self. Unfortunately, Meyer didn't have the flair of his dapper young friend. He couldn't walk the walk or talk the talk, and when he tried, he got himself in trouble.

Meyer first attempted to play white knight to a Madison Street prostitute named Sarah Ginsberg. He had already struck up an acquaintance with her, running errands and handing out her business cards. He was tough enough to handle the business side of the service, but his powers of persuasion failed him when he tried to get her to pay him for protection. Persistence didn't help either. The 16-year-old Sarah, who was already paying the local beat cop for protection, had him charged with annoyance. Meyer was fined two dollars — and now had a criminal record.

In less than two weeks, Meyer was back in court, this time charged by another prostitute, Lena Friedman, with disorderly conduct. According to the court record, Bugsy Siegel was also present at the time of this incident. Fortunately for Meyer, the presiding judge found the conflicting testimony of all parties so confusing he dismissed the case.

Soon after, Meyer gave up on this aspect of his criminal career. He was no believer in "third time lucky" — he already knew too much about the laws of probability. Instead, he concentrated on his strengths.

Meyer's contribution to his group was two-fold: he was the planner for joint ventures, and he was the banker. He convinced the boys that, while their individual activities were fine, there were occasions when working together produced bigger profits and greater safety from the law. Together, for example, they could swarm a store. Several boys could enter a store, quickly grab an abundance of pre-planned goods, then flee. Accomplices outside could innocently obstruct anyone who pursued them. This way, they could steal more, steal better goods, and run little risk of capture.

Meyer's "bank" tightly welded the group. All the boys were living with their parents, who wouldn't look kindly on their criminal pursuits. It was one thing to band together for school, recreation, and even self-defense, but committing crimes together was unconscionable. So the boys had to hide their money and spend it without their parents' knowledge. Meyer persuaded them to pool their money, with each member dipping into it only with the approval of everyone else. The money was also to be used to finance joint activities.

With the surplus money built up in their bank, the boys began running floating crap games. These games had to work fast because they were run on sidewalks and alleys controlled by adult hoodlums. The boys would set up their game, run it for an hour or two, then quickly move it to a different location.

Occasionally, however, the owners of the territory would catch up to them and a brawl would ensue. Soon the teenagers garnered a reputation for using force more effectively than their adult counterparts. By 1916, with the reputation had come a name: the Lansky-Siegel Gang.

Generally, Meyer was regarded as the brains of the gang and Bugsy the muscle. Both youth were underestimated. More than brains were needed to pal around Delancey Street with the gamblers, grifters, hookers, and hard men. While

Bugsy's aggressiveness may have overshadowed Meyer's seeming calm, Meyer had some toughness of his own.

Indeed, if his toughness was ever doubted, he dispelled this doubt before he even left school. Like almost every boy, Meyer had his share of schoolyard scraps — name-calling, grappling, wrestling on the ground, sometimes a fat lip, black eye, or bloody nose to show for it. But on the Lower East Side, the scraps could escalate to a more serious level of violence. The level to which a combatant was prepared to take this violence determined his reputation.

In the spring of 1914, Meyer showed just how prepared he was. Once again, a *cholent* played a prominent role. Alone at the time, Meyer was hurrying home on a Saturday with the *cholent*, still piping hot from the bakery, when he was confronted by a gang of Irish boys looking to terrorize him, perhaps worse. Meyer recognized the leader and recognized, too, that a Saturday afternoon prank born of boredom could become something much worse very quickly. A knife was waved in his face.

Meyer reacted instantly. He slammed the hot *cholent* on the head of the knife wielder with such force that the bowl shattered, cutting the thug's face and saturating his head and shoulders with boiling hot stew. The thug fell screaming to the sidewalk, and as he did, Meyer attacked his companions like a dervish, fists and feet flying, teeth flashing. He managed to pick up the knife and slash two of them before he was disarmed and overpowered.

Meyer had no chance to defend himself. Beating him to the ground, the older Irish boys attacked with fists and boots, intent on crippling him. Luckily, he was saved by a police patrolman who had heard the screaming of the injured knife wielder. Except for the first casualty, who required hospitalization for his facial cuts and burns, the Irish boys fled. Meyer managed to stagger home while the police tended to the injured youth.

For the second time, Meyer had failed to bring home the *cholent*. This time, however, he gave his mother money from his gambling profits to buy food and replace the broken bowl. She did not question where he got the money, and he did not volunteer the information. Nor did she question his battered, bloody state and his torn clothes. Life for Jews on the Lower East Side beggared such questions; best sometimes not to ask, better not to know.

Had the Irish gang had better relations with their Sicilian peers, they might have been advised to steer clear of Meyer. Obviously Meyer's confrontation with Salvatore Lucania earlier that year had not been mere bravado. He had been prepared to fight.

Just as Meyer was a lot more than a bookkeeper with a penchant for gambling, Bugsy Siegel was more than just a loaded gun looking for a target. He often proved himself bright, cunning, and open to reason. Doc Stacher called Bugsy "just about the nicest guy you'd ever want at a party" and, other than Meyer, "the best guy to have sit in on a planning session ... when the two of them were working together, there was never a problem that couldn't be handled."

Before Meyer was 17, the gang was augmenting their floating crap games by buying into other, more stable games. In effect, they were playing with the "big boys." They also branched into some strong-arm work for local loan sharks and other businesspeople on the gray side of the law. Pilfering from the backs of trucks was replaced by hijacking the whole truck; warehouse raids and burglaries replaced fruit stand thefts. Boosting Ring-Dings from the candy store escalated into collecting protection money from the candy store owner.

The Lower East Side was a small world, but a hothouse, nevertheless, where a young criminal population was growing and multiplying. The Lansky-Siegel Gang was an example of this phenomenon. The Italian and Sicilian gangs were another, notably that of Salvatore Lucania. No one could foresee what would occur if the Jews and Sicilians decided to agree on certain issues or, more importantly, what would occur if the two united in pursuit of their common interests. As it turned out, that process of unification began long before the Lansky-Siegel Gang was officially formed. It started as early as 1914, when Meyer was only 12 years old.

Chapter 3
What's a Friend For?

The course for the rest of Meyer's life was set in 1914. First was his encounter with Salvatore Lucania that winter. Then came his brawl with the Irish gang in the spring. Throughout that period, Meyer had also become a familiar face at the sidewalk crap games. His reputation as a hard-nosed streetwise youth was growing even though he was only 12. Then, that summer, Salvatore re-entered his life.

Summer days on Manhattan streets were hot and muggy. Relief came from opening the fire hydrants or, for the kids of the Lower East Side, swimming in the East River. The Manhattan shoreline was not yet completely clogged with piers and warehouses; there were still a few places where kids could simply crawl under a fence and sprint across empty lots or storage yards to reach the riverbank.

Here, at these few swimming holes, Jews and Sicilians — and occasionally the Irish — would put aside ethnic differences and disputes to cool off and have some fun. There were still fights, but they were relatively harmless skirmishes. The Irish kids loved to steal swimmers' clothes, enough of an irritation that swimmers would post a guard.

However, on one occasion, the Irish wanted more than a little harmless fun. The gang had not forgotten the *cholent* incident, and they chose the river to exact their revenge. Meyer and some of his friends were already in the water when the Irish gang showed up. Along with the Jewish boys were several Sicilians, including Salvatore, but the two groups weren't bothering each other. After all, it was a big river, plenty of water for everyone. Besides, it was too hot to fight. Then, quite suddenly, it wasn't.

Shedding their clothes and jumping into the river, the Irish contingent headed straight for Meyer and his group. Even before the groups clashed, the shouts of the Irish made it clear their intentions were beyond the usual skirmishes. The boy guarding the clothes was knocked flat, got up, and scrambled into the river for safety among his pals. The Irish boys followed, pouncing on the Jews.

The Jewish boys were giving as good as they got, but the Irish had numbers and size on their side. They weren't just dunking their opponents, they were holding them under, all the while brutally punching and gouging them. Weakened, choking, the Jewish boys were being overwhelmed.

Whether they just liked a good fight or whether Salvatore decided the enemy of his enemy was his friend, the Sicilians weighed in on the side of the Jews. The reinforcements should have settled the outcome, sending the Irish boys running. Instead, the Irish gang continued to fight, slowly being backed toward shore, where everyone could find footing. The ferocity intensified. A knife came out, a scream drowned out the shouting and cursing, and the water around the Irish gang leader turned red. His thrashing spread the stain wider.

The combatants knew one of them had crossed the line. As the gang leader's body slipped under the water, everyone — Sicilians, Jews, and Irish — fled to dry ground, tossed on their clothes, and disappeared into the streets. The gang leader's body was pulled from the river the next day.

Before the body was even autopsied, police jumped all over the case. An Irish youth had been murdered and the police force was predominantly Irish. The force's discrimination against the Sicilians and Jews in disputes involving Irish people was a part of life in the district. Soon, the police had a fair idea which boys had been present at the fight, but after that, the investigation hit a wall.

They were stymied by witness testimony, or rather, its vagueness. No one admitted knowing who had wielded that knife or even that there was a knife. Some suggested the victim may have hit his head on a rock or dove onto a sharp object. Others suggested he was a lousy swimmer who simply got caught in an undertow that dragged him through rusted junk on the river bottom. Those who were there admitted only that they were so busy looking out for number one they weren't paying attention to what others were doing. Speculation leaned toward Salvatore as the guilty party. He already had a reputation in the neighborhood for being as willing and capable of taking care of business himself as he was designating it to others. Nevertheless, the murder remained forever unsolved.

More significant than who did what to whom was the event itself: it was the first time Italian and Jewish street groups had acted in concert in New York. Even more noteworthy, it was the first time Meyer and Salvatore had shared common criminal cause.

Violence escalated after the East River incident. The Irish gangs aligned more forcefully against the Sicilians and the Jews. Later that year, Salvatore and Meyer met privately to plan action, defensive and offensive, against their enemies.

In his mid-teens, Salvatore had already quit school and now lived alone in a rented room. Although estranged from his parents because of his criminal activities, he was doing okay for himself. In addition to a job as a messenger, he was making good money from criminal business. This made him something of a hero on the Sicilian side. Meyer, with his success at gambling, and now his friendship with Salvatore, was the same on the Jewish side.

Salvatore's room became his and Meyer's favorite

meeting place — their improbable accord was initially a sore point for some members of their respective groups. Eventually, other members put aside their differences and joined the meetings. For the Jewish boys, all of whom lived at home, Salvatore's place was like a clubhouse, and Meyer provided the access. Moreover, everyone in the two groups was involved in petty crime. Finding common ground in mutual interests, the Jewish and Sicilian boys were soon involved in joint ventures.

During the next few years, Meyer and Salvatore became tight. They developed a strong mutual respect — both were tough, both were leaders, and both were loyal to their circle. Salvatore began going by the name Charlie Luciano, partly because it was easier for Meyer and his friends to pronounce. Though Meyer's gang was little more than a loose-knit bunch of Jewish neighborhood boys, the core of the future Lansky-Siegel Gang formed during this period, as did Charlie's Sicilian gang.

In 1916, shortly after he left school and took the job as machinist in the tool and die shop, Meyer's loyalty to his friend Charlie was put to a conclusive test. Charlie had capitalized on his job as a messenger by dealing drugs, purportedly selling opium by the bottle. Lower East Side drug traffickers had concocted a wicked brew laced with opium that could be sold by the swig, four swigs to the pint. As he went about his messenger duties, Charlie was selling it by the swig. Given that success, and the great cover afforded by his job,

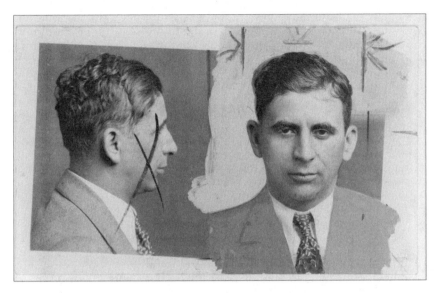

An early mug shot of Meyer Lansky

traffickers recruited him to make deliveries to other dealers. That's when the wheels fell off Charlie's wagon. He was
arrested for heroin possession. In quick time, he was sentenced to a term at the Hampton Farms State Penitentiary.

Charlie knew he'd been ratted out. So did Meyer. They
even knew who had done it — an Irish teen who'd been on
the losing side of the East River incident three years earlier.
The teen was also the son of a cop, which made revenge a
little dicey. But Meyer was more concerned with getting his
friend out of jail anyway — revenge could wait.

To that end, Meyer approached Max Goodman, Charlie's

Jewish employer. Goodman took up the cause, as much because he liked his former messenger as the fact that Meyer had interceded. Goodman visited the prison frequently, preaching calm and good behavior. He used his influence to obtain an early parole hearing for Charlie and went out on a limb to vouch for him, guaranteeing a job if he was paroled. Six months into his sentence, halfway, Charlie walked out Hampton's front gate. It would be 20 years before he saw the inside of a prison cell again.

Meyer's loyalty sealed the deal with Charlie. They met immediately after the latter's release. Likely, Charlie didn't thank him for his efforts. By then, the pair were very like-minded. That they would help each other was taken as a given by both.

Of course, neither had forgotten the matter of the "Mick rat." Charlie was all for dealing with him immediately, but Meyer laid out the reasons why that would be a big mistake: "Do it now and your door'll be the first one the cops kick in. Even if they couldn't prove anything, they'd pull your parole. Don't forget the kid's old man is a cop."

Nearly 13 months later, the "Mick rat" disappeared from the streets. Police turned the Lower East Side upside down searching for him or a rat who might have information. Throughout the investigation, they harassed Charlie constantly, but Charlie had been out of town, sheltered in an unshakable airtight alibi. No rat came forward, and no body was found. No one thought to ask a "matchstick-thin" Jewish teenager what transpired. Not that it would have done any good — Meyer took his silence on this matter to his grave.

Chapter 4
The Chosen Few

From the time he was 12, Meyer hid his other life from his parents. At home, he continued to be the model of a dutiful eldest son. He attended heder, ran errands, and went out of his way to help his mother. When he turned 13, he bar mitzvahed.

Meyer's parents knew of the dangerous and criminal opportunities the streets presented, but they hoped their eldest son would be among the majority of immigrant Jews and sidestep that. Meyer hadn't. Rather, he'd immersed himself in it because, as Doc Stacher put it, "he was a lot sharper than the average Joe, and damn well knew it." Plus, he was learning fast.

At first, Meyer thought his shrewdness alone could make the wheels go round. He had figured out how to beat the sidewalk crap games, and the operators put up with it as long as he didn't win too much at any one time. As a periodic winner, Meyer was in one sense a shill for them, enticing other players to throw down their money. "Hey, if a scrawny kid can do it, I can, too!"

As Meyer and his group diversified their activities, he saw that intimidation supported by violence could make the wheels go faster. This was useful knowledge, but in his mind it made him little more than a street punk, one hustler among thousands — okay for a kid, but Meyer intended to be a lot more than just another mug hanging around crap games and saloons 10 or 15 years down the road. He intended to be a boss, and for that, he realized, one more ingredient had to be added to the mix — immunity, which came only through bribery. In Meyer's teen years, when he was running floating crap games, he noticed that beat cops would regularly roust his games, often running right past the established games to get to his, partly because he wasn't making payoffs. Whether it was the cop on the beat, the judge in court, or the politician in city hall, there was always someone on the right side of the law with his hand out, willing to provide services or look the other way for the right price.

As for the involvement of higher-ups of the Lower East Side power structure, Meyer had only to walk two blocks from home to get the message. Meyer lived on the 400 block of Grand Avenue. In the 200 block was Fat Al Levy's Downtown Merchants Club, the classiest gambling den on the Lower East Side. Fat Al provided high stakes poker, no limit craps, blackjack, bookmaking, and roulette — his club ran 24-7 and was never raided. Had it ever been raided, the customers found inside would have been a true cross-section of the district's movers and shakers.

From outside, Meyer would watch a steady procession entering Fat Al's every night. There were lawyers, judges, top cops, union bosses, merchants, manufacturers, stockbrokers, and Tammany ward heelers — all of them with fat cigars, custom suits, beautiful women, and chauffeured cars. The glitterati also included the men who ran serious crime in the district, from established crap games, bookmaking, and loan-sharking to providing protection on the docks and in the garment and longshoring unions.

Seeing these people socialize together didn't surprise Meyer. He remained especially unfazed by the mingling of the crime bosses with the Tammany ward heelers. For decades, very little had happened in New York City that did not have at least passing approval from Tammany Hall, the political machine of the city's Democrat Party. The machine drew its power from its ability to deliver the immigrant vote. It achieved this by controlling men in certain jobs — municipal officials such as building and health inspectors, police, and firemen — and by granting favors and "arrangements." The ward bosses had tremendous power over average citizens, and their fingers were in many pies, some of them corrupt.

The youths working with Meyer and Charlie started a

pool of funds, a percentage from each of their operations, to be used for bribery purposes. At first it was very small and wasn't really required. Later it grew to massive proportions, all in the care of Frank Costello, whose role in the group was "greasing the wheels."

Although Fat Al's world was far removed from that of the teenaged Meyer, Meyer and Charlie were still doing well. Between 1917 and 1920, their respective gangs grew in numbers and became comfortable working with each other. All the members were busy in many of the Lower East Side's marginal rackets. Sometimes together, sometimes separately, Meyer's and Charlie's gangs looted warehouses, rolled drunks, ran or guarded crap games, strong-armed for loan sharks, and acted as "schlammers" in labor disputes. Schlamming consisted of wrapping a piece of pipe in cloth and bludgeoning a victim. (The term is thought to have derived from the Jewish name for the rag trade, *schmattes*, and "slam" which is frighteningly self-explanatory.)

Meyer's and Charlie's were the men in the trenches who helped make other people's criminal schemes work. They had their fingers on everything happening on the streets. Young, ambitious, and ruthless, they were primed to take advantage of every opportunity that presented itself and had acquired a reputation for effectiveness. They were also capable of rebuffing any incursion on their interests.

In mid-1920, Meyer had a run-in with Joe "the Boss" Masseria, an up-and-coming Unione Siciliane underboss who had brought a reputation to New York as the Unione's number one assassin in Palermo, Sicily. The Unione Siciliane was a powerful, centuries-old Sicilian criminal organization that now flourished in many U.S. Sicilian immigrant communities. Masseria, trying to muscle in on Meyer's crap games, had his goons break up a game, viciously beating Meyer's workers. Shortly after, Meyer retaliated. Perhaps on information supplied by Charlie, who was working off and on with the Unione Siciliane, Meyer and Bugsy learned the name of the leader of the Masseria group's raid. The man was waylaid and crippled.

Masseria did not bother Meyer's games again, although he had the manpower at his disposal to wipe out the entire Lansky-Siegel Gang if he chose. Rather than having been scared off, Masseria moved on to more lucrative business, notably booze.

In January 1920, the Volstead Act had become the law of the land. In the interests of clearing the path to enhanced family values, improved quality of life, and a reduction in alcohol-fueled lawlessness, the Volstead Act prohibited the manufacture and/or sale of alcoholic beverages throughout the United States. Temperance advocates trumpeted their victory. Meanwhile, drinkers scrambled for other sources of liquor. As it turned out, these were remarkably easy to find. Masseria helped out, as did thousands of others already active in the underworld, including Meyer and Charlie.

With the Volstead Act, the Lansky-Siegel crew quickly

found that its reputation for efficiency and violence was exactly the ticket for obtaining work riding shotgun on liquor loads for bootleggers. For Bugsy, it was like the Wild West — a dull run for him was when he couldn't shoot at someone. For Meyer, it was all workaday, except the money was better, and as far as he was concerned, it was all about money.

By then, Louis Buchalter had moved over to Brownsville to pursue protection and labor rackets. Dutch Schultz was across the river in Brooklyn, starting a business to supply beer to speakeasies. Doc Stacher had moved to New Jersey, where he was getting along with gambling involvements. And Longie Zwillman was also in New Jersey, doing very well in the liquor trade. Everyone kept in close touch, still sharing some projects and profits. Meyer's "old gang of mine" had not so much gone their own ways as expanded the gang's overall operations.

Then, in early 1921, Meyer received a dinner invitation he couldn't refuse. He dressed in his best and headed uptown, alien country to him in those days. The joints uptown were more glamorous and inaccessible than even Fat Al's.

Meyer was just 18 years old the evening the maître d' in Park Central Hotel escorted him across the hotel's dining room to the table where his host waited. Meyer's steps were soundless, absorbed in plush carpet. Overhead, massive chandeliers lost their light in damask wall hangings and lushly upholstered mahogany chairs, catching back some of it in glinting fragile crystal, heavy silverware, and pristine linen tablecloths. No aspect of the elegant setting escaped Meyer's notice. He was on the home turf of Arnold Rothstein, a man who had been his idol for several years. As he sat down to dinner he had some hopes, but he still didn't know why he'd been called.

Rothstein was a professional gambler, by reputation the high rollers' high roller. And more. He owned a piece of many of New York's finest nightclubs, restaurants, and gambling houses. He could comfortably rub shoulders with society's elite — indeed, they sought him out for their chic soirees and dinner parties — or with lowlife thugs in the seediest pool halls and back rooms, if there was enough money involved to interest him. He could work a stock market fraud with ease and often did. It was said of Rothstein that he could offer odds on a dead man breathing again and have the corpse come to life long enough to collect from the bettors.

When Chicago White Sox players offered Rothstein first crack at rigging the 1919 World Series, he turned down the deal. It was too risky. In his estimation, they'd surely get caught. He was right: the scandal still taints the national pastime. Nevertheless, Rothstein cashed in on that World Series. He was sure someone would be stupid enough to front the players. Already knowing what was bound to happen, he simply bet accordingly. No one became America's "King of the Gamblers" without being at least a little wily: reduce the risk, maximize the edge.

Rothstein was cultured, dapper, and handsome. In

the language of the time, he was a "cake-eater," an "egg," a "swell," and definitely "swank." What it came down to was that he was a ladies' man who lived the good life. Part of his charm was his profession and its aura of illegality. In most parts of the United States, gambling was against the law. Rothstein acknowledged his profession and had the presence — the image — to make it not only socially acceptable but something to be envied. Behind his facade of well-to-do trappings, however, was a mind honed to calculate odds and opportunities. Meyer was all ears that historic night at the Park Central.

Rothstein started out by telling Meyer a few things the young hoodlum already knew. First, a lot of money could be made supplying illicit liquor, whether it was retailing it at speakeasy counters or selling it wholesale to speakeasy owners. Next, he told Meyer that the Sicilian crime bosses thought they already had a monopoly on the trade because they'd been able to access the hundreds of Italian households that had operated closet stills for years. Meyer already knew that, too, but this was just Rothstein's preamble.

Then he got to the point: the crime bosses didn't think big. They were going to miss the boat, literally, even though they thought they already had a gold mine. Rothstein criticized their myopic business sense and ethnic xenophobia, particularly their anti-Semitism. "They never leave their neighborhood," he noted, "because even a minnow can feel like a big fish in a small pond and they want everyone to think they're big fish." Meyer could understand that. Already, he and Charlie were reaching out into New Jersey, Brownsville, Brooklyn, and the Bronx — wherever they could make money. To them, the size of fish didn't matter; they were looking for bigger ponds. Rothstein commended their capacity to not only put aside ethnic prejudices but also grow stronger from their convergence.

Rothstein had a plan to "forget the closet stills." He wanted to start selling the genuine article — imported by boatloads from Canada, the Caribbean, and Europe — to markets that had real money: the middle class, the swells, the nightclubbers — in short, the people who could and would pay a premium, if not for the liquor itself, then for the label on the bottle.

Somewhere between the Chateaubriand steak and the baked Alaska, Rothstein described in detail his established contacts with distillers worldwide, ship owners and ship builders, and people in high places who would always be looking the other way (for a price, of course). In short, he had the resources to get high-quality liquor to the shores of America.

Perhaps it was when the men enjoyed post-dinner coffee, cognac, and cigars that Rothstein described his problems and suggested his solution. The main problem was getting the liquor from the ships to the shore and into the marketplace. He talked about the need for a team that would make the payoffs at the ship's rail, off-load the liquor from the ships, load it on trucks, distribute it to pre-arranged buyers, and collect the money. The people doing that had to be trustworthy and efficient. They also had to have muscle and a willingness to use it when necessary.

Rothstein's proposition, then, was that Meyer and Charlie together provide the infrastructure for operations in New York and New Jersey, as well as the servicing of any out-of-state customers whose shipments were coming through the New York area. Rothstein, as often was his custom, would simply put the wheels in motion and occasionally apply some grease. Meyer had no doubt of the man's ability to do this. But it remained for Meyer to present the proposition to Charlie.

He didn't need to use a hard sell. Charlie agreed to the plan immediately, and soon New York's fabled Rum Row was born. Rothstein was true to his word. By 1922, Atlantic waters outside the international limit along the coasts of New York, New Jersey, Rhode Island, all the way north to Maine and south to Virginia, were lined with cargo ships laden to the gunnels with thousands of cases of first-class liquor. Gin, scotch, and Irish whiskey arrived from the British Isles; rye came down the coast from Canada; vodka, champagne, and fine wines arrived from Europe; and rum came north from the Caribbean.

At night, coastal waters were filled with the roar of engines as speedboats transshipped the liquor to waiting fleets of trucks. More often than not, gunfire also rattled across the water. The U.S. Coast Guard pursued the speed-boats as best it could, and the two often engaged in gun-fights. With the Coast Guard obviously overwhelmed by the sheer number of rumrunners, the government sent in the U.S. Navy with its heavy machine guns and cannons. The flow of liquor was unabated.

More dangerous to the rumrunners were hijackers. Some were freelancers, but most were hirelings of rival boot-leggers attempting to steal one another's consignments. In these confrontations along Rum Row, many boats were literally blown out of the water.

Meyer frequently rode the speedboats out to the waiting freighters. Meanwhile, "Red" Levine, one of his toughest men — later to become an apparently fearless, certainly ruthless, killer — refused to step on a deck and always pleaded with Meyer not to make the trips. There is no evidence that Meyer got a rush out of speeding across water without lights in the pitch dark. More likely, he made those trips because he carried Rothstein's purchase and order books in his head. As well, he was carrying the cash to pay for the load. Just as important, he didn't want to be shorted by the seller in the count or the quality of the liquor.

Meyer also still rode the trucks with Bugsy to spray would-be hijackers with hot lead, but the Lansky-Siegel loads almost always reached their customers. During this period, Meyer carried a gun at all times, as did everyone who worked with him. Bugsy may have been the gang's foremost shooter, but Meyer, safe to say, was always guarding his back. Rothstein guaranteed buyers the best, and Meyer made sure they got it. The profits surged in like a tidal wave.

Like any good businessman, Meyer was tuned to the opportunities inherent in spin-offs from the main profit center, the bootlegging. By the end of 1922, in partnership with Bugsy, he opened three speakeasies in the Lower East Side. He could supply the best booze on a regular basis, so why not to his own joints?

With the spectacular profits from rum-running, Meyer needed other places to invest his money. He began buying control of established street crap games, always using middlemen to maintain arm's-length involvement. Some of the games were in the Lower East Side; others were in New Jersey under the knowledgeable trusted guidance of Doc Stacher. But, surplus money just made more money.

Meyer then put together a pair of small-time gambling houses, profitable in themselves, but made more so because his patrons could always buy a drink. These establishments were unnamed, anonymous, and bare bones, known only to gamblers in their local neighborhoods and operated in the secretive manner of speakeasies. The money multiplied, none of it particularly legal.

As the cash flowed in, Meyer realized he needed to have a legitimate livelihood, at least for the record, in the likelihood he might someday be asked what he did for a living. He knew he had to distance himself from illegal money or, if he couldn't do that, explain its source. By then, Meyer and Charlie had both given up the pretence of holding down regular jobs — they were far too busy.

A legitimate business was one thing, but Meyer couldn't see taking a loss on an investment. That would have been like working for nothing, or worse, losing money he'd already earned. Rothstein had been moderately successful legitimating his money, but that money had come from quasi-acceptable sources (gambling), and Rothstein had always distanced himself from outright thuggery. He sank his surplus into real estate, gambling facilities, the stock market, and racehorses. Some of these investments had made him money, while others were costing him a bundle. Meyer didn't want to take a flyer into unknown territory. Losing that first nickel had been enough for him — no more gambling based on imperfect knowledge.

Meyer looked hard at potential spin-offs from the bootlegging — aspects of the overall process that could be profitable and appear to be legitimate, but aspects with which he felt comfortable. Ship owning crossed his mind, but this was beyond his budget. The speedboats were a possibility, but they were shot up or crashed too often to be cost-effective. So Meyer settled on trucking.

In partnership with Bugsy and another member of the group, Moe Sedway, Meyer opened a car and truck rental agency on the Lower East Side. Buying a fleet of vehicles, outfitting a garage for their storage and maintenance, and hiring mechanics and other staff was a considerable but safe and respectable investment.

The new business was an immediate success, with the fleet transporting liquor throughout the eastern United States, even as far away as Detroit and Chicago. The company mechanics kept the vehicles in perfect running condition and customized them to carry as much liquor as possible. If police happened to confiscate a loaded truck, Meyer could disclaim any responsibility. "I only rent out the truck," he could argue. "What the renter does with it is none of my business." Of course, the drivers were working for him or other rumrunners — his vehicles' reputation for mechanical reliability had created widespread demand.

While Meyer was busy handling Rothstein's shipments arriving on Rum Row, Charlie was busy at his end of the operations. Able to use his connection to Joe Masseria's crime family, Charlie could bypass Rum Row and unload freighters directly onto the New York City docks. Organized crime already controlled many comings and goings along the waterfront, exercising its control through labor unions and the Unione Siciliane's far-reaching corruption of police and Tammany Hall officials. Being a Jew, Meyer couldn't use this approach — Joe the Boss would never have permitted it.

This was not the last time Meyer and Charlie took separate routes to the same destination. Diversification of activities became a pattern for them. They each carried on doing what they did best, utilizing whatever unique resources happened to be available. Many times, however, they teamed up in joint ventures, one of the reasons the pair was so formidable. For example, both were adept at hijacking — they could orchestrate a hijacking as quick as anyone else in the trade, and if a few dead or wounded were left in the aftermath, well, that was part of doing business.

Meanwhile, Meyer's education in gambling took a quantum leap forward. By 1927 he had established his style of ownership. On paper, he appeared to own nothing other than a percentage of the rental agency. He kept the details of his activities in his head. Street corner crap games, floating crap games, and other gambling that operated in hotel rooms, back rooms of speakeasies, pool halls, and restaurants — in these he would hold an interest but never appear to be the front man.

His responsibility was the operational organization and the money. The people who worked with him always received a fair share, just as the people who gambled in his games always received an honest deal. In an environment heavy with greed, intimidation, and distrust, Meyer found honesty to be a virtue. In later years, people who didn't trust their own grandmothers with a dollar trusted Meyer with millions.

By example, Rothstein taught Meyer a corollary lesson: where gambling was concerned, there was no need to cheat because the house always won in the end. Meyer's passions for arithmetic and the probabilities in various gambling games resulted in his being able to determine the house edge with astonishing accuracy. His years around gambling also enabled him to pinpoint crooked dealers and cheating customers with relative ease. By the mid-1920s, Meyer and his partner, Doc Stacher, had a nucleus of expert dealers and crap table managers working for him in numerous operations. Then Rothstein invited him to become involved in New York State's premier casino mecca, Saratoga Springs.

Each year since 1920, Rothstein had "owned" Saratoga Springs for the entire month of August. It had been the custom in New York State for several decades to throw open Saratoga Springs to high-rolling gamblers from across America for that glorious month when the thoroughbreds were racing. Every August, gambling was as uninhibited as it could possibly be in a state where it was illegal but sanctioned by payoffs.

To accommodate the influx of the country's most serious gamblers, the staff of the best gambling houses in the area were recruited. Meyer's and Doc Stacher's were among these. So were some of Frank Costello's. Frank, who owned the Twenty-One Club and Copacabana, among pieces of others, closed down his clubs for the month to move his staff to Saratoga Springs, maître d's included. Costello was also a member of the inner circle that was becoming known as the Luciano-Lansky Gang.

The magnitude of the month's gambling handle was suggested by the size of Saratoga's United States and Grand Union hotels. Although they did serious business only in August, they were the two largest hotels in the world. In addition, scattered on the outskirts of Saratoga were "lake houses," all of which provided fine gourmet dining and elegant gaming facilities. Up to 1928, Rothstein ran the entire show, subcontracting for all services.

Initially, Meyer provided professional dealers, croupiers, pit bosses, and floor managers to Rothstein's August enterprise. Working under the arm's-length aegis of Rothstein, Meyer learned every aspect of running a casino — the future Las Vegas style of casino, for that was the sum of the Saratoga Springs operations. He learned everything from counting the towels to toting the daily take, toting up wastage and breakage in the dining rooms and bars, placating losers, and booking entertainers.

Eventually, Meyer established his own lake house, called Piping Rock. His two principal partners were Frank Costello and Joe Adonis, both of whom went on to become major organized crime bosses in New York and New Jersey, respectively. Each August, Costello provided catering services and staff from the Copacabana for Piping Rock. Adonis provided the best table crews and equipment from his New Jersey gambling houses. New York City high rollers could enjoy some familiar comforts of home. A third partner, Frank Tierney, had the local connections to ensure everything ran hassle free.

As for Meyer, he was the day-to-day CEO. He was a full partner in Piping Rock, but, as had become his custom, his name did not appear on documents. Instead, his brother

Jake's name was listed in its place. This was the first time Jake stood as Meyer's proxy.

Meyer's management style at Piping Rock was summed up by one of his dealers: "'Inconspicuous' is the word. You didn't even know he was there, and when he was there, he looked like nothing." This would have pleased Meyer. It was exactly the persona he wanted to maintain.

Chapter 5
Wedding Bells and Warfare

The 1920s were more than financially good years for Meyer Lansky. It was also during this decade that the unassuming little man from the Lower East Side fell in love.

Meyer was so discreet in his relations with the fair sex that only his two closest friends, Bugsy and Charlie, knew who he dated. He was never seen at the Copa with a showgirl on his arm, and his car was never seen parked in front of a mistress's apartment building. Just as he kept business separate from family, with the exception of Jake, he kept his love life separate, too.

In late 1928, he announced that he was engaged to be married to a girl he'd known since childhood. Anna Citron was the daughter of Moses Citron, a produce dealer based in

Hoboken and a long-time friend of Meyer's father. Meyer had been dating her for some time, often going on double dates with Bugsy and a friend of Anna's, another neighborhood girl.

Anna was devoutly Jewish, devoted to Meyer, and a good cook — the precise qualities Meyer's mother had hoped he would find in a wife. The Lansky family was very happy with the match. To satisfy his future father-in-law, Meyer finally became a naturalized American. Unfortunately, in his haste to get this bit of bureaucratic business out of the way, he neglected to note his criminal record on the forms, an omission that would later haunt him.

As far as both the Lansky and Citron families knew, Meyer was in the auto rental business. They also knew he "dabbled" in what Meyer sometimes called "the liquor supply business," but this was hardly considered a sinful sideline — by then, almost everyone seemed to be involved in some aspect of it, either as a supplier or a buyer. Shortly before the wedding, Moses Citron offered Meyer a position in his produce firm. Meyer, always anxious to shore up his ostensible legitimacy, accepted.

Meyer and Anna wed on May 19, 1929, in a ceremony attended by the full families on both sides. Only one outsider was invited — Charlie Luciano. His presence was a measure of the bond between the two men.

Meyer went to work for Moses, if only part-time. Most of his time was spent on gambling and liquor-related work. Nevertheless, he quickly became an asset to the produce business. Moses's business had never been better. Meyer also helped start several other food-related businesses, including Molaska Corporation Inc., a company that would presumably manufacture powdered molasses as a sugar substitute. Actually, Molaska was a front, engaged in distilling bootleg whiskey. Interestingly, Moses Citron bought into the company with a $120,000 investment.

On the home front, Meyer's marriage quickly became rocky, despite Anna's getting pregnant. In fact, the early pregnancy may have contributed to their marital unrest. It set up a conflict for Anna between Meyer the family man with a wife and child and Meyer the serious criminal. During their courtship, she had become aware that Meyer was involved in criminal activities with Bugsy. She knew, for example, that their auto rental business was a front, but didn't know to what extent. Presumably, she'd hoped that, once married, Meyer would settle down.

He didn't. He still carried a gun, and he held meetings with other gun-toters at his house. He was away from home most of the time and paid only lip service to Judaism. Anna wanted her husband to shape up. She tried to reason with him; she tried tears, raging, and throwing things. But Meyer shouted back. He also threw things, and he demeaned her in public.

Nevertheless, to neutralize Anna's concerns, Meyer strove to reinforce his marriage. He tried spending more time at home and working longer hours in Moses's produce business. Still, despite his efforts, he couldn't help but wish that Anna would keep her concerns to herself. "Why can't she be like your Italian friends' wives?" he complained to Charlie and Doc Stacher one night. "They know their place; they stay at home and never question what their husbands are doing."

Meyer's stressful home life was an unwanted distraction, to say the least. His conflicts with Anna came at a time of great unrest among gangsters. By 1929, a deadly gang war had erupted in New York City, and Meyer and Charlie were caught squarely in the middle. Even Bugsy had noticed Meyer's preoccupation, cautioning him, "Now is not the time to take your eye off the ball."

The war had been coming for a long time. On one side was Joe the Boss Masseria, an overweight man driven by greed. His cruelty was as legendary as his flash temper, which flared whenever he felt his importance as a Unione Siciliane boss was slighted. His organization, which numbered in the hundreds, was active in gambling, prostitution, extortion, loan-sharking, bootlegging, and about any other vice that turned a dollar. He despised competition, dealing with it by taking it over or, failing that, eliminating it.

Masseria was considered an old-guard Unione Siciliano, a "Mustache Pete," reminiscent of the traditional dons in Sicily. The Mustache Petes obtained their name from a late 19th-century fad among men to sport elaborate handlebar mustaches as symbols of importance. While the Mustache

Meyer Lansky

Petes in the American Unione Siciliane no longer grew such facial hair, they had other distinctions that set them apart from the younger gangsters who proliferated in the 1920s.

For the Mustache Petes, ethnic and family loyalties ran deep. Masseria, for example, distrusted anyone who was not a native or not related to a native of Palermo, Sicily, his hometown. He would work with non-natives, but only if they were Sicilian and only if they could be controlled. Mustache Petes also tended to localize their activities, treating a defined neighborhood as a fiefdom. Here they could be lords and masters, and be seen to be the lords and masters. To them, the Unione Siciliane was more than a business or career arrangement, it was an institution laden with tradition, regulation, authority, and respect.

To the extent that Mustache Petes were men of the neighborhoods, their younger counterparts were men of the world. Charlie and Meyer epitomized the youthful perspective that transcended ethnic lines. To them, business was business, and if making a profit required dealing with non-Sicilians (or non-Jews), so be it. In business, they endorsed no Old World traditions, although they did exploit them, and to some extent respected the importance in which they were held by others. Charlie, being Sicilian, particularly had to cater to them. Meyer had only to be aware that a part of the Unione tradition was anti-Semitism.

The thorn in Masseria's side was an upstart named Salvatore Maranzano. Maranzano was a well-educated native

Sicilian from the village of Castellamare Del Golfo. He was also the protégé of one of the most powerful Mafia dons in Sicily and had been sent to America for the express purpose of becoming the Mafia boss of the United States.

Maranzano's Sicilian connection was influential enough to keep Masseria from outright attack for a while. The younger man used the time wisely, building an organization comprised mostly of ambitious young men from his hometown. Prohibition helped the process immensely. It provided hundreds of thousands of dollars in working capital, money that could be put back out on the street to finance more criminal activity.

Both bosses wanted Charlie Luciano's allegiance — and his bootlegging business. They also wanted him to cease working with the Jews (the Lansky-Siegel interests). As early as 1924, Masseria's people began pressuring Charlie by hijacking his liquor shipments. Charlie took it in stride, giving as good as he got. Bugsy Siegel and others from the Jewish group — including Red Levine, Louis Buchalter, and Dutch Schultz — beefed up shipment security and periodically hijacked Masseria's loads, just to let him know their displeasure.

In 1929, after much discussion, Meyer convinced Charlie to work out a compromise with Masseria. Charlie agreed to work with Masseria against Maranzano, provided Charlie's own operations stayed outside Masseria's control and provided he could continue working with Meyer and his Jewish group. This last point was non-negotiable.

By then, Charlie and Meyer were partnered in many bootlegging-related enterprises. From Rum Row, they were shipping liquor to cities as far west as Minneapolis-St. Paul. As well, they were still pooling money in Frank Costello's "bribery bank," a fund the groups had set up to finance the suborning of public officials — Costello was the group's liaison to officialdom. In short, between their intertwined businesses and their close personal friendship, Charlie and Meyer simply would not put the passing of control on the bargaining table.

For a while, Masseria saw the light, but eventually it dimmed in the shadows of his greed and anti-Semitism. He renewed his demand for Charlie to dump the Jews and turn over his bootleg operations to Masseria's control. To make his point, he put out contracts on two of Charlie's key men.

When Bugsy got the news, Meyer was at home helping Anna through her pregnancy, a case of momentarily having his eye off the ball. True to his volatility, Bugsy immediately wanted to start what would have been a suicidal shooting war with Joe the Boss. Fortunately, Meyer found out before Bugsy could get a crew together. He reined in his friend and, through Charlie, worked out some concessions to pacify Masseria. They relinquished control of a handful of Dutch Schultz's less profitable speakeasies and some of Frank Costello's bookmaking locations.

By October 1929, the Masseria-Maranzano conflict had escalated to open warfare, a protracted bloodbath that became known as the Castellammarese War. Up to this point, Charlie and Meyer had been able to avoid most of the violence, letting the two crime bosses decimate each other's ranks. Then Maranzano set up a meeting with Charlie, ostensibly to discuss a peace. The two men were to meet alone. Only Meyer could have dissuaded Charlie from attending, but he could not be reached. Charlie hadn't called him, as normally he would have, because he knew of Meyer's problems at home.

The meeting was a trap. While accounts differ as to what happened to Charlie, two things were clear: He was beaten nearly to death, among his injuries a knife slash down his cheek, the scar he carried to his grave. And Maranzano offered him a position as his number two man, provided he kill Masseria. Charlie refused.

When Meyer heard the news the next day, he termed it the worst moment in his life. "If I'd been around," Meyer later recalled, "Charlie would never have gone on that lonely ride. When Maranzano nearly killed him."

After the attack, the men who worked for Charlie and Meyer suddenly seemed to disappear from the streets of New York. In reality, the game was afoot. While strong, the Lansky-Luciano team wasn't strong enough to take on both Maranzano and Masseria. So, once Charlie was released from the hospital, they decided to exacerbate the war between the two bosses. They began selectively picking off important lieutenants in both camps, including Masseria's chief bodyguard, always ensuring blame went to the opposite warring faction.

While Meyer may have been involved in putting these pieces into play, tragedy struck his family in January 1930. His first child, Bernard (later nicknamed Buddy), was born crippled. Anna blamed her son's condition on Meyer's evil lifestyle: the defect was "the wrath of God." Initially doctors diagnosed Buddy's condition as cerebral palsy, but later, it was deemed a spinal birth defect that probably occurred while Buddy was in the womb.

Shattered in spirit, Meyer disappeared from New York soon after his son's birth. Charlie finally located him at a hideaway near Boston and dispatched Vincent Alo — a.k.a. Jimmy Blue Eyes — to support Meyer through the crisis. While Charlie was undoubtedly worried about Meyer, the motives behind this dispatch went much deeper than merely wanting to help a friend in need. Meyer's presence during the group's criminal councils was essential. He carried details of the group's transactions, schedules, and financial affairs in his head. Beyond the barest minimum of legal requirements, his "carved in stone" rule was to commit nothing to paper. Equally crucial to the group was Meyer's cool head and almost Machiavellian ability to sort through a problem and devise a strategy for dealing with it. Not just for Bugsy was Meyer the voice of reason.

What happened between Meyer and Jimmy Blue Eyes during their time together is conjectural. One story has it that the men put away a lot of whiskey while Meyer seesawed with his emotions. Another story, speculated by law enforcement figures, was that Meyer was a drug addict who went cold turkey. This is unlikely because Meyer was a man who controlled his emotions — he probably would not let drugs compromise that control, certainly not to the point of addiction.

Whatever the case, after about a week of seclusion, Meyer rose one morning, cleaned himself up, ate breakfast, and drove back to New York, almost as if nothing had happened. But something had. Jimmy Blue Eyes was Meyer's friend and confidant for the rest of his life, even acting as his nominal executor upon Meyer's death.

After Buddy's birth, Anna Lansky was beside herself, overwhelmed with a baby and needing Meyer's support at home. By then she loathed his gangsterism so vehemently that it drove their every conversation. During his weeklong "time out," Meyer had apparently resolved in his own mind how he would deal with the domestic conflicts. He immersed himself in his work, ignoring Anna's endless rants.

By this time, the Castellammarese War had spread into other cities. Rival Unione Siciliane bosses were choosing sides. Masseria had also taken to bringing killers into New York from other cities. While Charlie continued to keep a low profile, Meyer hit the road like a traveling salesman, visiting his customers. He visited criminal contacts in Boston, Cleveland, Detroit, Chicago, Philadelphia, Pittsburgh, New Orleans — everywhere he and Charlie sold liquor. At every stop, Meyer preached Charlie's (and his) philosophy of profit:

there is enough for everybody, so let's live and let live.

Meyer and Charlie were men of vision. They had seen enough of the fiefdoms of the Mustache Petes. In their view, organized crime wasn't organized. They believed criminal activities should be coordinated nationwide. Certainly there should be local control of local activities, they said, but there should also be an overriding group of leaders — not just one man — to ensure local groups could take advantage of national opportunities. Second to this vision was a cessation of debilitating, costly internecine warfare between and within groups. Not only did it get in the way of making money, it drew unwanted public scrutiny. Cooperation rather than competition, Meyer preached to his customers, was the only path to future success for everyone.

Meanwhile, Joe the Boss remained confident of his ultimate victory in the war. By 1931, he had killers on the street that Maranzano's people wouldn't recognize until it was too late. Plus, he had Charlie in his camp, a man whose hatred of Maranzano he assumed had to be vengeance-driven, and whose loyalty had been well demonstrated by increasing Masseria's profits and providing effective ideas in the ongoing war.

In reality, however, Masseria was losing the war even though he was holding his own against Maranzano. He did not realize that Charlie and Meyer had decided the time was right for them to weigh in more overtly — they would get rid of Joe the Boss once and for all.

Masseria's operations were ripe for takeover. Charlie now knew them in detail and, as Masseria's number two man, he also knew his personnel firsthand. The latter were receptive to Charlie because as he increased Joe the Boss's profits, he increased those for the rank and file. Another deciding factor for Charlie and Meyer was Masseria's persistent greed — he still coveted Charlie's liquor interest. Of course, he also still wanted "those Jews" out of business.

In April 1931, Charlie and Meyer made their move. On the 15th, Charlie set up a morning meeting with Masseria to lay out a plan to deliver a coup de grâce to Maranzano. Masseria was all ears. The details of Charlie's plan are unknown, but the meeting lasted into late morning, which meant Joe the Boss applied his own cunning and chipped away at its loose points. Still, Masseria's questions were no match for Charlie's gift of the gab. By lunchtime they were in agreement on the details, elated. Not only had they come up with a way to end the war, they'd also secured a means for capturing Maranzano's substantial interests and ensuring the ascension of Joe the Boss to de facto national boss of the Unione Siciliane — definitely cause for celebration. Charlie proposed a sumptuous lunch at one of Masseria's favorite eateries, Coney Island's Nuova Villa Tammaro. As befitted Joe the Boss's prestige, Charlie would pick up the tab.

The lunch was a tremendous success. The men ate and drank from shortly after noon until around 3:30 p.m., then settled back for a last round of coffee and a few hands of cards. Charlie excused himself to go to the restroom and "iron his shoes" — the meal had messed with his fragile digestion. He lingered awhile, and when he emerged, Joe the Boss was as dead as a squashed maggot. Other than his corpse and Charlie, the restaurant was deserted.

Charlie called the police, who descended on the scene in quick time. Masseria was on the floor, partially shrouded in a blood-soaked tablecloth. Six bullets were eventually dug out of his corpulent body, 14 more out of the floor, table, and walls. Charlie seemed in shock, but not the least embarrassed to tell the press that the call of nature probably saved his life. Those 14 slugs that missed Joe could have been in him. Charlie had seen nothing, heard nothing, and knew nothing. Neither had the restaurant owner, who, lucky for him, had been taking a stroll to enjoy the sunny spring afternoon.

The police fussed and bothered. The newspapers went wild for an edition or two, until the paparazzi ran out of gory photographs. Rumors abounded, but the murder went unsolved.

In fact, Joe the Boss had been set up — the plan against Maranzano was a sham. A few days earlier, Charlie and Maranzano had met at the Bronx Zoo, where Charlie laid out Joe's fate, with the provisos that Maranzano would make no effort to take over Charlie's and Meyer's interests and that Charlie would manage Joe the Boss's empire on behalf of Maranzano.

The shooters that afternoon were rumored to have

been Albert Anastasia, Vito Genovese, and Joe Adonis from Charlie's faction, led by Bugsy Siegel from Meyer's side. Another rumor circulating was that Charlie and Meyer had worked late the night before making sure the getaway car was tuned up and in tip-top shape.

Salvatore Maranzano was naturally delighted with the outcome. Ostensibly, Charlie had finally done his bidding, and, accordingly, Maranzano made Charlie his number two man.

Maranzano promptly called a meeting of Unione Siciliane men from throughout the state. Meyer called it "an emperor anointing." Charlie, who attended the grand gathering in the Bronx later said, "The only thing missing was a crown. I looked everywhere for it. But his chair was bigger than everyone else's and he sat on it like a throne. He gave us a long lecture and talked for what seemed like hours about Julius Caesar and stuff like that." As had become custom, the Jewish gangsters were not invited.

Maranzano declared himself "the boss of bosses" at that meeting, and everyone pledged obedience, each man doing so individually, and each man handing Maranzano a tribute envelope. The tribute in total may have been as much as a million dollars in untraceable cash. Maranzano then explained how New York City would be divided into five "families" and set up a hierarchy that would be the structure for organized crime for years. It remained for him now to bring the other cities in the country under his control.

Meyer and Charlie had their own ideas. The pair had agreed that both Masseria *and* Maranzano had to go. There was no place in their grand scheme for the old ways, notably the notion of a boss of bosses. The elimination of Masseria had been only the first step. Now they would turn their attention to Maranzano.

Meyer, accompanied by Bugsy and an entourage of bodyguards, toured the country again, this time recruiting anti-Maranzano Jewish gangsters. Simultaneously, Charlie planted spies within Maranzano's inner circle, not difficult now that he had a central role in the organization. Among his recruits were many of Maranzano's household staff and two of his underbosses, Joe Bonanno and Joe Profaci.

Charlie's task was relatively easy because Maranzano had broken a cardinal tradition of the Unione Siciliane — he'd failed to share that cash tribute with his men. Given its enormity, that was cause for serious resentment. As a result, Charlie knew when Maranzano got up in the morning, when he went to bed, and what he did in between. He also knew his plans.

Charlie reached out to Italians and Sicilians in other parts of the country to form alliances as well. Young bosses in Ohio, Pennsylvania, and Florida came on board. Mo Dalitz and John Scalise committed to Charlie's plan. So did Al Capone's outfit in Chicago. Some may have bought Charlie and Meyer's grand scheme, but more likely they were frustrated by Maranzano's delusions of grandeur and angry that they were expected to pay tribute in exchange for nothing.

Meyer and Charlie asked for nothing but peace if and when they took care of business in New York. They described opportunities and options for everyone, and they keyed on mutually profitable cooperation without a boss of bosses. Everyone would cut their own inter-city and interstate deals, which could be coordinated through the aegis of a nation-wide group. This "Commission" would be made up of the main bosses from across the country, all of whom would have equal voice in decision making. Local territory and authority would be left intact. Just as important, egos would also be left intact.

Their scheme was coming together so well that perhaps Charlie and Meyer were a little overconfident and a little too public. At any rate, Maranzano caught wind of it, and the cunning old don drew up a death list. Charlie and many of his people were on it. Curiously, only a single Jewish name made the list — that of Dutch Schultz. Like Masseria before him, Maranzano had completely underestimated the strength of the Jewish gangsters. He failed to realize that in New York and other cities Jewish gangsters provided the muscle and some-times the brains to their Italian and Sicilian counterparts.

Charlie's spies saved his life. They had obtained a copy of the death list and found out Maranzano's plan. Charlie would be called to a meeting at Maranzano's upscale Park Avenue office, where he would be whacked by Vincent "Mad Dog" Coll, a contract killer imported from Chicago. At last, the Jewish guns would be popped out of the woodwork. Charlie and Meyer decided to strike Maranzano at his office. Presumably, if it was good enough for Charlie's demise, it should be good enough for Maranzano's.

The seed for the execution plot had been sown months before. Five Jews were chosen for the mission, and their designated leader, Red Levine, was Meyer's most trusted and experienced bodyguard and driver. The five were taken off the streets and, in seclusion, carefully coached in their roles. Meanwhile, Meyer had his brother tip the Internal Revenue Service (IRS) that Maranzano's accounts for his real estate company were suspect.

Although Maranzano had clean books, he'd become used to IRS agents periodically dropping into his office to scrutinize them. He was always accommodating, and his staff had orders to be on their best behavior when the agents showed up. In addition, Maranzano felt invincible, confident he knew on sight every gangster in New York City who could shoot straight. This confidence was just the weakness Meyer and Charlie were looking for.

On September 10, 1931, four men entered Maranzano's outer office, identifying themselves as IRS agents. Maranzano was in the reception area at the time talking to a lieutenant, Tommy Lucchese, who was actually a Luciano confederate sent to finger the boss. Knowing the drill when the IRS came to visit, Maranzano's bodyguards and staff politely welcomed them. Maranzano put on his best smile. At a nod from

Lucchese, suddenly the guns came out. The bodyguards were quickly disarmed and lined up against a wall. Maranzano was taken to his private office. Here, two of the killers stabbed and shot to death the completely surprised "boss of bosses." All Maranzano's workers immediately saw the wisdom of pledging loyalty to Charlie. Only Mad Dog Coll publicly swore vengeance. A few months later, Bugsy Siegel took care of that nonsense. Mad Dog died in a hail of bullets while placing a call from a phone booth in Manhattan.

The transition across the country to the Charlie-Meyer method of doing business was seamless because the pair had already laid the groundwork. Still, they again embarked on a nationwide tour to reaffirm their philosophy, this time traveling together. When they got to Chicago, Al Capone, though sinking fast, gave them a heroes' welcome. Hundreds of gangsters, including Jews and other non-Sicilians, assembled to hear Charlie's message. Generally, they liked what they heard. Some older Mustache Petes grumbled a little, but, remembering Maranzano's grandiose "boss of bosses" ceremony, they were impressed that Charlie refused tribute when it was offered.

Now, presumably, Meyer could focus more attention on his abiding passion, the gambling business. In fact, throughout the turmoil and the perilous juggling of vendettas and violence, he had never put it on the backburner, but he hadn't had the opportunity to expand it as quickly as he would have preferred.

Chapter 6
Dimes to Dollars

Throughout the 1920s, illicit liquor was Meyer and Charlie's financial mainstay. Slowly, however, more and more of their surplus money was being directed into gambling and, to a lesser extent, loan-sharking.

By the time Arnold Rothstein had given the men their crack at Saratoga Springs, Meyer and Charlie, along with Frank Costello, Joe Adonis, Doc Stacher, and others of the group, were established in gambling. Their holdings included gaming rooms, street games, slot machines, and bookmaking in New York and New Jersey.

Their bookmaking operation alone, overseen by Frank Costello and Vito Genovese, had more than 200 pushcart vendors taking bets for them. They used ice cream vendors in summer and hot chestnut vendors in winter. They used milk, bread, and ice deliverymen, rag and bones collectors, fruit and vegetable men. These men collected the bets and passed them to shopkeepers. The shopkeepers were provided telephones and paid a salary to phone the bets in to the banks set up in the neighborhoods. The system spread throughout the New York boroughs and supplemented, by hundreds of thousands of dollars, the fragile subsistence-level incomes of poor New Yorkers.

In 1925, Meyer and Charlie were enjoying some R & R at the opening of the original Beverley Club in Covington, Kentucky. The Beverley was very posh, offering all the usual amenities, including gambling for high rollers and otherwise well-heeled. Both men enjoyed gambling for pleasure. Meyer, especially, loved the sounds of gambling — the rattle of dice dancing across a felt-covered crap table, the ball bouncing into a slot on the roulette wheel, the snick of cards being dealt from a six-deck card shoe, the rise in player chatter if someone was on a hot streak.

While taking a break from the tables, watching the glitz and big money crowding the club, Meyer had a thought: "What about the little guy who can't even bet two bucks on a horse, but would like to bet on something? Ain't he entitled, even if he can only bet a couple of pennies?" He turned to Charlie. "Suppose a guy could bet on a number every day. If enough people bet only pennies, we could afford to make the odds high enough for them to buy the idea that any day of the week they could hit for a big bundle." The pair began to discuss the idea.

Back in their hotel suite with a quart of whiskey and a couple of scratch pads, Charlie and Meyer spent the night working out the mechanics. They could pay off odds of 600 to 1 when a number was hit, but actual odds of it being hit were 1000 to 1, a very substantial guaranteed margin for the house.

When they returned to New York City, they talked up the idea to some of their partners. The others laughed at a plan to go after pennies when everyone else was reaping dollars. Eventually, however, Charlie and Meyer persuaded Costello to try it out through his Harlem pushcart-shopkeeper operation, a kind of test market.

The response was overwhelming. Soon it seemed everyone in Harlem was playing a daily number. Just as Meyer and Charlie had predicted, pennies became dollars, and then thousands of dollars. Suddenly the skeptics wanted a place at the trough. The numbers racket, or policy, as it is sometimes called, was born. To this day, it is a major moneymaker for organized crime.

The success of the numbers racket brought Charlie and Meyer a secondary benefit: steady income for their rank and file, their "soldiers." Moreover, it was far less hazardous than riding shotgun on a liquor truck or strikebreaking. The money instilled loyalty. Even back then, Meyer and Charlie were looking after their people, building allegiance for the future.

Dimes to Dollars

Within a year of Meyer's concerted systematic integration of the numbers racket into small betting operations, they were grossing a million dollars a week. Charlie owned a substantial percentage of the business, but he left the complexities to Meyer and Costello.

While their gambling enterprises flourished during the mid- to late 1920s, Meyer and Charlie missed out on the start of another gambling phenomenon known as carpet joints. In some respects, the carpet joints were like the lake houses of Saratoga Springs, but most were not quite so refined. Joe Adonis ran a popular one in New Jersey that was in an old barn. The carpet joints were roadhouses, usually located on highways just outside major cities, sometimes just over a county or state line from its customer base. They catered mostly to the middle class, offering food, drink, dancing, sometimes a floor show, and, discreetly, adjacent to the main room, gambling. Many had a touch of class — a doorman, a maitre d', and carpets on the floors (hence the name).

The Covington Beverley Club was a high-end carpet joint in Kentucky, just over the state line from Ohio. The Beverley was in Kentucky because officials there were more conducive to ignoring its operation than officials in Ohio. Several other carpet joints were busy in Bergen County, New Jersey, across the George Washington Bridge from New York City. Bergen County officials saw "community benefits" that New York officials felt weren't in New Yorkers' best interests. The New York public didn't feel quite the same way. Many used the shuttle service provided by club owners to cross the bridge for evenings of fun and games. Unfortunately, Meyer and Charlie were too busy to put the time and energy into developing their own carpet joints.

In 1929, however, almost by accident, they got in on the ground floor of another spectacular gambling opportunity that could be worked right into their existing operations. In May of that year, newlyweds Meyer and Anna went to Atlantic City for their honeymoon. So many "well-wishers" showed up from across the country that two hotels were fully booked. Anna did not realize it, but Meyer and Charlie had used the honeymoon as a cover for a council of crime bosses. The priorities of the gathering were ways to improve efficiencies in the bootlegging business and plans for activities when Prohibition ended.

The Mustache Petes were not invited. Still, New York City was well represented by Meyer and Charlie, Dutch Schultz, Frank Costello, and Albert Anastasia. From Philadelphia came Waxie Gordon and Nig Rosen. Moe Dalitz was there from Cleveland, along with his people. Abe Bernstein represented Detroit's murderous Purple Gang. The list went on: Al Capone, Longie Zwillman, Joe Adonis, Frank Scalise, and more. These were the men keeping the liquor flowing down the throats of thirsty Americans. Discussions, seminars, workshops, and conferences were conducted while playing golf, strolling on the boardwalk, participating in penny-ante stuss games, or sunning on poolside chaise lounges.

Meyer, throughout, hammered away, promoting his own passion — gambling.

Al Capone brought along Moses Annenburg, a Chicago associate who had a proposition. Before the Atlantic City meetings ended, Meyer, Annenburg, and a third man, Frank Erickson, had worked out a tentative arrangement. Erickson was Arnold Rothstein's former right-hand man. In partnership with Costello, he had a "model bookmaking operation" in New York City. Erickson brought to the table the bookmaking expertise he'd learned from Rothstein and the idea that the New York model could be replicated nationwide. Meyer had nationwide connections already in place thanks to liquor distribution, and he had access to a great deal of money.

Annenburg brought the clincher. He controlled a wire service that could transmit results from any horse race in the country to betting joints willing to pay for the service. He was looking for investors and contacts who could finance spreading his wire service to bookmakers nationwide.

The wire-service deal was made-to-order for organized networks of bookmakers. But before they started using the wire service in New York, Erickson added a couple of embellishments to local bookmaking practices. First was the laying off of heavy bets to protect payouts. In other words, bets would be spread around so that no individual bookmaker had to take a serious loss. Second was another move to ensure laying off bets would be timely — past-posting, a system whereby race results came in slightly late. Knowing the results of a race five minutes before they were received by bookies could earn thousands and also quickly put obstreperous bookies out of business. This practice wasn't new. In the past, bookies would sometimes have confederates at the track telephone results to them before they could otherwise be obtained. With access to Annenburg's wire service, past-posting could be much more refined.

Having secured the nickels, dimes, and dreams of poor people, Meyer and Charlie turned their attention to the more extravagant illusions of the wealthier people. With the wire service in full swing, they set up horse parlors all over New York. The well-heeled could saunter into an atmosphere of plush comfort, free drinks if one was a regular, and recognition even if one was just an occasional gambler. The atmosphere encouraged action — betting cages like those at the racetracks, a wall-to-wall tote board, and bustling clerks ever changing the chalked-up odds and results coming in from all over the country. The scene on a busy afternoon rivaled the controlled chaos of the New York Stock Exchange floor, a few blocks' walking distance from the Lower East Side. Just as Meyer had predicted, whatever a jockey's colors when the horses started from the gate, they always won for Meyer.

During his years of poverty as a child, Meyer could not have foreseen a time when he would have *too much* money. Yet, by the late 1920s he did, and so did many of his associates. From bootlegging alone, government officials estimated Meyer and Charlie were probably each grossing $4 million to \$5 million a year between 1925 and 1930. How to hide this money but still use it continued to be one of Meyer's major problems.

At first, Meyer funneled much of the money into legitimate and quasi-legitimate businesses in the United States. Many other crime bosses had done the same, more as a front than to hide income from the tax man. Real estate, food processing and distribution, garment production, and restaurants were popular choices. One gang boss controlled New York City's ice distribution — a major industry in pre-refrigerator days. Another owned a florist shop. Joe Bonnano owned a funeral parlor. None of this was enough; the enormous amount of money coming in outstripped their means to secrete it.

It would be a crime kudo for Meyer if it could be said he'd invented money laundering. However, money laundering — investing dirty money in clean businesses — has likely been around since the money economy came into existence. What Meyer did was find a new home for dirty money — the anonymous, numbered Swiss bank account. From there, dirty money could be used as collateral for legitimate bank loans, and the cash from the loans could then be funneled back into investment in the United States.

In the space of a few years, Meyer moved beyond utilizing offshore banking to cleanse Mob money; he also used it to pay bribes to highly placed officials who helped clear the way for gambling licenses and other activities.

The importance of bribery to the success of Meyer and Charlie, their associates, and their criminal rivals from the beginning of Prohibition into the late 1930s cannot be underestimated. Their reach was such that they contributed substantially to the 1928 presidential bid of former New York State governor Al Smith on the Democrat ticket. Their support was also a measure of the influence they had with Tammany Hall, and although Herbert Hoover won the election, Meyer and Charlie didn't give up.

In 1932, they decided to become "lobbyists" at Smith's second run for the Democratic presidential nomination at the party's national convention in Chicago. This time, Meyer, wanting to hedge their bet, had feelers sent out to Franklin Roosevelt's camp to ensure whichever Democrat won the nomination, the Mob would have an influential foot in the door.

Meyer, Charlie, Frank Costello, and Longie Zwillman were part of the East Side contingent that traveled to Chicago with the New York Democratic delegation. With the exception of Meyer, who orchestrated efforts from backstage, the group worked the convention's floors doggedly. They ran 24-hour hospitality suites, called in old markers, and tried to establish new ones. Roosevelt appeared to be looking like a winner, and after extricating a promise, though not face-to-face, that he would be "kind" — the word Meyer used to his biographer, Uri Dan — they went full tilt on FDR's behalf.

Roosevelt won the nomination and the election.

Promptly, just as Prohibition was repealed in early 1933, he initiated an anti-crime campaign aimed at destroying the mob and Tammany Hall. The new president of the United States was serious. New York City's colorful mayor, Jimmy Walker, was forced to resign and scampered off to Europe to avoid prosecution. Even Jimmie Hines, FDR's own point man inside Tammany Hall, ended up in jail.

Meyer took it in stride. "Philosophically," he told Uri Dan, "in a way I guess it was to be expected. When you become President of the United States you do your duty. I had no quarrel with Roosevelt for taking action against crime or what he and his law enforcement people said was crime."

Meyer's efforts to secure a mutually beneficial relationship with Roosevelt may have seemed a bust, but as it turned out, he managed to turn a sow's ear into a silk purse. During the delegation, he had laid the groundwork with Midwest Mob contacts to expand gambling operations. Another, more far-reaching result of the Chicago trip was the coming together of Meyer and Louisiana governor Huey "the Kingfish" Long. In quick time, Meyer and his fellow New Yorkers found themselves fishing in the bayous. The catch was far more bountiful than anything law enforcement anglers in New York City were hooking at the time. But, then, Meyer was using better bait.

Negotiations with the Kingfish were opened in Chicago to put gambling into Louisiana in a big way. Meyer wanted exclusive licenses to put slots and other small money gambling games into bars, stores, and restaurants through-out the state. He also wanted exclusive licenses to develop upscale casinos, attractive enough to bring in high rollers from all over the United States. These were licenses except in the legal sense. The Kingfish was in control of state and local enforcement.

Meyer traveled to the Big Easy with Doc Stacher to final-ize the deal at a time when FDR had already ordered the IRS to go after the Kingfish. As soon as Meyer and Doc described the security of numbered Swiss bank accounts, adding that they could easily pump several million dollars of the free, untraceable money into the Kingfish's Swiss account, the deal was sealed — FDR be damned!

Under the statewide direction of a former Rothstein confederate, Dandy Phil Kastel, and the able support of his associate Seymour Weiss, Meyer set up operations in New Orleans. In one respect, the New Orleans casinos — the Beverley Country Club, named after the club in Covington, and the Roosevelt Hotel's Blue Room — were the harbin-gers of the Las Vegas to come. These establishments were pure class. Even Basin Street had to play second clarinet for a time.

By the end of 1933, Meyer may have been seeing the United States as 48 potential gambling hotspots, all his. First Louisiana, then expansion into Arkansas, followed by more casino operations in Kentucky. Meyer didn't slow down. He now wanted Florida, and California was also on his radar.

He'd had his eye on Florida since the earliest rum-running days, when he and Charlie were bringing liquor from the Caribbean via The Bahamas. Most of it came directly to New York's Rum Row; however, southern states were usually serviced through drops in Virginia, the Carolinas, and Florida. But for one hazard, Little Augie Carfano, Meyer decided the effort to set up gambling houses in Florida was worth the potential payoff. After all, he reasoned, the snowbirds of the north loved the winter warmth of the south, and they needed to do something during those long hot winter months ... why shouldn't they gamble?

Little Augie was Florida's crime boss, so soothed perhaps by warm Caribbean breezes and easy rum-running money, he'd grown less than hungry. Meyer and the East Side sharks didn't leap on Little Augie as they had on Maranzano. No voracious, high-profile, feeding frenzy here. Instead, Meyer quietly bought the Tropical Park racetrack. Then, he had Moses Annenburg bring in his wire service, but only for Lansky-owned and -controlled gambling houses and bookmakers. Meyer owned the turf before Little Augie discovered he'd lost it.

Only one of Meyer's Florida casinos ran into difficulty. He'd set it up in Broward County, on a parcel of land that had been zoned into lots. Citizens took offense at his establishment and obtained an injunction prohibiting a business on the lot. He was ordered to shut down. Overnight, Meyer moved his building to an adjacent lot not covered by the injunction. Quickly, he also began making substantial contributions to local charities, churches, hospitals, and libraries — a tactic he'd used successfully in Louisiana. Once again, it worked. He had become too valuable a citizen to run out of the county.

When the Volstead Act was repealed in February 1933, Meyer and Charlie made a smooth transition into their other enterprises. There seemed to be no bumps in the road ahead. So optimistic were the New Yorkers that Meyer convened a meeting of a select group in Charlie's Waldorf Towers apartment. Charlie and Bugsy were there. So were Moe Dalitz, Doc Stacher, and Phil Kastel. Meyer asked each to cough up $500,000 to bribe a dictator and set up a gambling empire in Cuba. What dictator in his right mind would say no to $3 million cash in a black bag?

According to Doc Stacher, when the bag was opened in Havana, Fulgencio Batista said nothing for a moment. Just looked. Then he turned and shook Meyer's hand. Batista was apparently in his right mind. The deal was struck. The Mob owned Cuba.

Chapter 7
The Politics of Crime

By 1933, the criminal structure Charlie and Meyer had built in New York City was at the pinnacle of its power. The Mob controlled New York's docks and major trade unions. Gambling, loan-sharking, and protection were still growth industries. Their interests and influence extended far outside New York.

The new U.S. president had done them no favors despite their support, but they wrote that off as a caveat emptor experience. Close ally Al Capone had been imprisoned in 1931, but his organization still seemed to be in capable hands. Capone's conviction for income tax evasion, as well as those that sent Moses Annenburg and a host of other high flyers to the cells for the same reason, were potentially nasty harbingers duly noted by Meyer, but he was confident that his own and Charlie's ducks were in a row. Some were, some weren't.

On the home front, the harsh bite of the Depression, contrasted with the public violence of the Castellammarese War, the flamboyance of some local crime bosses, and the blatant corruption of officials, was stirring an anti-gangster backlash in the city. Then, New York found its Eliot Ness. America's premier gossip columnist, Walter Winchell, dubbed him "Mister Crimebuster," but his real name was Thomas Dewey. He was driven by political ambitions that far exceeded his appointment as a special prosecutor with a mandate to root out corruption and crush organized crime.

Dewey was a young, squeaky-clean family man. His slim build, piercing eyes, and pencil-thin mustache gave him the look of a ferret. He received his first taste of public acclaim when he worked with Republican jurist Samuel Seabury, whose 1930–31 investigation of corrupt city politics so weakened Tammany Hall that another crime fighter, Republican Fiorello la Guardia, was elected mayor in 1933 and held the post until 1945.

With Tammany Hall on the run and a Republican mayor in power, Dewey was elected district attorney and given the authority to go after the gangland bosses. Putting together a hit list was easy for him, but somehow he missed Meyer. Indeed, Meyer's habit of always trying to operate in the shadows may have helped him escape notice. But he was also out of town much of the time on family as well as Mob business.

The Politics of Crime

In 1932, Meyer's second son, Paul, was born. Anna was still less than happy, still not reconciled to Meyer's business dealings — all she could say that was remotely positive was that he was a "clean fingernail man," presumably the equivalent of a white-collar worker. Meyer's two sons, and later a daughter, Sandra, locked him into his marriage. In any case, divorce was rare at the time, and many North American families stayed together for the sake of the children.

Nonetheless, Meyer's feelings for his family were genuine. Deeply concerned about Buddy's disability, Meyer embarked on cross-country treks, later with his family in tow, seeking advice from specialists. The odyssey included at least one trip to Europe. However, he was unsuccessful in finding the help he needed.

Dewey started his gangbusting campaign in early 1935 by publicly naming Dutch Schultz his first target. For months afterward, he applied constant surveillance, paid informers, made allegations in the media, and conducted systematic raids on Schultz's operations to bring the gangster to book.

The Dutchman was a stone-cold killer, but the pressure began to take its toll. He began to believe that Dewey's campaign was part of a plot by fellow criminals, including Meyer, to take over his rackets. Another gangster Dewey focused on was Bo Weinberg. Like Dutch, Weinberg had been a part of Meyer's Lower East Side faction since the early days. In October, Schultz panicked — he had Weinberg killed, a sure sign to those around him that he was losing his grip.

Schultz then went to the Commission and asked permission to put a hit on Dewey. The Weinberg murder had been bad; to kill a district attorney would have been devastating. Moreover, Schultz threatened that if he *didn't* get permission and Dewey or the mayor got their hands on him, he'd sing in any key they wanted to hear. Nevertheless, his request was denied. He stormed from the meeting, vowing to do it anyway.

For several weeks, Dutch kept Dewey under as intense a surveillance as Dewey had on him. Each day when Dewey left for work, he would pass a man pushing a baby in a carriage. The man and baby had become regulars on Dewey's morning route and, Dewey recalled years later, the two of them often exchanged "good mornings." The man was a Schultz killer, waiting for the phone call giving him the go-ahead to gun down Dewey on the street. Realizing Schultz was more of a loose cannon than they'd originally thought, the men of the Commission voted in favor of putting a contract out on him.

According to Doc Stacher, it fell to Charlie "the Bug" Workman, Mendy Weiss, and another Jewish compatriot to deal with the problem, which they did promptly. Dutch and three bodyguards were gunned down in Newark's Palace Chop House. Like Charlie during the Masseria assassination, Dutch was in the restroom. The Bug walked right on in and, with a single shot, ensured that Dutch was not as lucky as Charlie.

With Dutch dead, Dewey moved down his list, unaware

that the Mob had saved his life. On April Fools' Day 1936, Dewey named Charlie as the number one enemy in New York City. With that, he issued an arrest warrant for charges of "compulsory prostitution." On Meyer's advice, Charlie promptly fled to Owney Madden's Hot Springs resort in Arkansas to hole up while things cooled down, giving his lawyer, Moses Polakoff, and Frank Costello time to smooth things over.

But there would be no smoothing over. Dewey had lined up prostitutes and pimps prepared to testify that Charlie ran the biggest prostitution ring in the city, which he perhaps did. Polakoff was not optimistic, and Costello's courthouse connections had been largely purged after the Seabury investigations.

Dewey didn't idle his time while Charlie's people scrambled. Instead, he had the Arkansas State Police raid Madden's resort and arrest Charlie. He was immediately extradited to New York.

Given the daily publicity Charlie's trial received, it might as well have been held on stage in a Broadway theater. Prostitute after prostitute paraded to Dewey's witness stand to tell their stories of payoffs, threats, and sometimes beatings, all alleged to have originated from Charlie — remarkably unlikely because Charlie was well insulated and far removed from the daily round of individual prostitutes. Enough mud was thrown that some of it stuck. On June 7, 1936, Charlie was convicted and sentenced to 30 to 50 years in Dannemora state prison, still the longest sentence ever handed down for that charge.

Suddenly, Meyer's plate was very full. He was busy enough with his own affairs in Cuba, Louisiana, and Florida. Now Charlie placed him in charge of his financial and organizational responsibilities as well. With Meyer as his liaison, Charlie was able to continue his overriding influence on Mob business. No one in the Mob disputed Meyer's new power.

With the Dutchman dead and Charlie in Dannemora, Dewey had moved on to target another weak link — Louis Lepke Buchalter. A problem there could do more than simply touch on Meyer.

Lepke was another former teenaged Lansky associate, who had set up business in Brownsville. He'd started out under Rothstein's tutelage running the garment district protection racket. Soon, he had expanded his operations to other businesses. Enter Meyer and Charlie looking for something in which to invest bootlegging money. They proposed that Lepke funnel money or loans to garment manufacturers with the ultimate objective of becoming "partners" in the businesses. He suddenly had a chance to stop schlamming or burying anyone who disagreed with him and become sophisticated, using financial leverage and the velvet glove of gentle intimidation to reap his profits.

Unfortunately, Lepke couldn't resist bashing heads and burning factories to achieve his ends. Worse, he took his newfound profits and got into major drug trafficking. To Charlie and Meyer, this was a very bad move. But Lepke had breached more than the Commission's tenet against drug trafficking. He was withholding his share of money due Charlie for other involvements. Forget the laws of the nation — Lepke was breaking the Mob's laws.

In 1937, Dewey got his warrants, but Lepke had disappeared. With the help of friends, he managed to hide out for two years, but he was like an open sore to the Mob. Inevitably, Meyer was obliged to call a meeting of the Commission. Bugsy even came from California. He was all for "popping" Lepke on the spot — Bugsy's solution to most problems of this nature. Meyer did not agree. Instead, Lepke was coaxed out of his hideout and, not incidentally, his life.

"Friends" had convinced him that a deal had been cut with the feds: turn himself in, cop to a minor drug charge, and walk away with a lenient sentence. But it didn't quite work that way. Giving up in glory, Lepke was driven by Albert Anastasia and gossip columnist Walter Winchell to a clandestine meeting. Their car pulled up briefly behind another black sedan. Lepke switched cars, and Anastasia and Winchell sped away. In the back seat of the black sedan was Mr. FBI himself, J. Edgar Hoover, who formally placed Lepke under arrest.

Lepke promptly got 14 years for the drug charges, then was given up to Thomas Dewey and the State of New York. When state charges were settled, he was handed another 30 years consecutive. But Dewey wasn't finished. Lepke was linked to a 1936 murder of a shopkeeper. Reminiscing, Doc Stacher said, "To be quite honest, we were sorry for Lepke, who had been the victim of his own stupidity and who was now completely crazy as far as we could see. However, there's not much room for sentiment in these matters."

In March 1944, Lepke, along with Mendy Weiss and Louis Capone, was executed in Sing Sing's electric chair. To date, Lepke remains the only major organized crime figure ever executed by the state.

After the Schultz and Charlie problems and during Lepke's long ordeal, New York's mob kingpins kept their heads down. Business continued very much as usual, though more discreetly. Dewey continued to prowl the fringes of the rackets. He came close to the top only once more. This was when he landed killer Abe "Kid Twist" Reles and turned him into an informer.

In another Dewey show trial, Reles was to testify against a number of men who were alleged to be members of Murder, Inc, Dewey's name for the Commission's internal enforcement wing. Before he could testify, however, Reles plunged to his death from his sixth-floor hotel suite, where he was being kept under 24-hour police guard. His demise saved Bugsy Siegel and Albert Anastasia from probable murder convictions. As always, Meyer's name never came up.

Chapter 8
Meyer Goes to War

M eyer Lansky would never have made it in vaudeville as a song and dance man, and a comic he wasn't. If he did a pratfall, no one would laugh, and a pie in the face was unthinkable. However, during the late 1930s and the World War II years, Meyer's juggling act was definitely star quality.

Throughout the late 1930s, Meyer was busy developing gambling operations across the United States and in Havana. His Molaska Corporation now had several plants in three different states, distilling thousands of gallons of liquor for the bootleg market that popped up after Prohibition, when the government imposed high taxes on legal booze. He had to move these plants regularly in order to stay ahead of government agents.

Through a company named Emby Distributing, Meyer owned the Wurlitzer franchise to supply jukeboxes in New York, New Jersey, Maryland, and Connecticut. Then, of course, there were the problems caused by Thomas Dewey's continuing crusade against crime, to say nothing of having to keep an eye on Charlie's interests.

Not to be forgotten was Meyer's family. For some time, to facilitate Buddy's treatments, Meyer lived in Boston and commuted regularly to New York City and other locales across the country. While the Hotel Nacional was being set up in Cuba, he also lived for several months in Havana, even taking his family there for an extended vacation. Meyer had hired good help for his Havana operations. In a curious turnabout, the man he hired to run the Hotel Nacional was his former neighbor, Fat Al Levy, who decades before had run the elegant Downtown Merchants Club on Grand Avenue.

As the normal everyday world of a "clean fingernail man," all of this should have been more than enough to juggle. But it was also around this time that Meyer added another dimension to his life, a dimension that in a sense went all the way back to Grodno, his birthplace.

Pro-Nazi sympathizers, known as Bundists, were rabble-rousing in New York City, conducting meetings and marches with the intent of inflaming anti-Semitism. They invariably encountered opposition — attempts to shout down their speakers, disrupt their marches, and occasionally incite brawls.

Meyer took more than a passing interest. He assembled his own group of "concerned citizens," probably never more than two dozen, but all tutored in head cracking and bone breaking. They added their numbers and expertise to the anti-Bundists, with Meyer himself sometimes actively participating in the group's attacks.

For Meyer, this was one of his few bragging points, particularly one incident. Walter Winchell had tipped him off that top American Bundist Fritz Kuhn was to give a speech in Manhattan. "We got there that evening," Meyer recounted to Uri Dan, "and found several hundred people dressed in their brown shirts. The stage was decorated with a swastika and picture of Hitler ... There were only about 15 of us but we went into action." Meyer described how his "concerned citizens" threw firecrackers and started fights, transforming the meeting into a near-riot. Kuhn never did get to speak that night. Meyer, on the other hand, got his message across.

On December 8, 1941, the United States entered World War II. Meyer registered as a machinist with the Selective Service Board, though at 39 years old, he was unlikely to be called up.

Throughout 1942, Nazi U-boats made a mockery of the U.S. Navy's attempts to protect shipping on the Atlantic Ocean. Then, in December that year, the French liner *Normandie*, being outfitted as a troop ship, was burned at the dock in the Port of New York. Albert Anastasia, not only a power on the docks but ardently pro-Mussolini, was so vocal in his approval of the arson that some suspected he had a hand in it — yet another unresolved allegation. Sabotage by Nazi agents or sympathizers working on the docks was, nevertheless, probable.

There were also suspicions that Italian sympathizers were somehow tipping off U-boats when convoys left New York. Despite efforts by its 150 agents assigned to port security, U.S. Navy Intelligence could not penetrate the docks. It needed to find a better way, and it needed to do it fast because the Port of New York was the main embarkation point for supplies and troops headed for the battlegrounds.

The port had never been busier. Normal commerce was almost at a standstill. The docks teemed with troops assembling in the shadows of heavy guns, tanks, and thousands of crates and pallets of munitions. In addition, warehouses bulged with more supplies. A vast army was on the move.

Laid by, clogging the Hudson and East rivers, were ships either waiting to be loaded or waiting for convoy strength and destroyer escorts to build in numbers for the trip across the North Atlantic. Authorities were well aware of the potential for a disaster far more destructive than the munitions ship mishap that caused the 1917 Halifax Harbour Explosion, which killed 2000 people and injured 9000. Moreover, the mysterious *Normandie* fire made it clear that the port was vulnerable to saboteurs.

Realizing that the Mob controlled the port through the International Longshoremen's Association (ILA), and that members of the association would talk only with Mob approval, Navy Intelligence took a circuitous route to obtain this approval. First, it went to District Attorney Frank Hogan, who sent officers to Thomas Dewey, the newly appointed governor of New York. Dewey assigned Murray Gurfein, one of his most knowledgeable investigators, to make the initial contact with the crime bosses.

Gurfein met with Joe "Socks" Lanza, who ran Fulton's Fish Market, presumably because Lanza was connected. He was — he knew Frank Costello and Joe Adonis. Gurfein pitched Lanza to have his people help identify suspicious strangers and Nazi sympathizers in the market and among the fishing fleet. Lanza stalled him — no problem for Gurfein because he knew Lanza would have to pass the request up the line for authorization, and up the line was where Gurfein wanted to go. Gurfein was also aware that Lanza knew Charlie Luciano. And Dewey's people were fully aware that even in Dannemora, Charlie still ran New York City. In order to ensure a meeting with Charlie, Gurfein made it clear to Lanza that if he didn't follow up on the proposal, the district attorney was prepared to move on the seven outstanding extortion and conspiracy charges racked against him. Lanza decided to do the patriotic thing.

Not only did Lanza know Charlie, he also knew Meyer, and he owed the pair a heavy debt — they had helped clear him of a murder charge in the early years by encouraging witnesses to admit their forgetfulness. Lanza first went to

Meyer, and together they met with Frank Costello. The three men agreed not to make a move unless Charlie gave the nod. Meanwhile, Gurfein also approached Charlie's and Meyer's lawyer, Moses Polakoff, asking him to intercede with Charlie. Polakoff deferred until he could meet with Meyer.

Meyer and Polakoff needed no drawn-out discussion of the request. Both immediately saw in any deal the opportunity to help Charlie get out of prison. Charlie's first question would be "What's in it for me?" — a fair question considering the length of his sentence and the state's apparent intention to keep him in Dannemora, a horrendously antiquated prison called Siberia by its inmates.

At a breakfast meeting, Polakoff, Meyer, and Gurfein began to work out the elements of a deal for Charlie. After the meeting, Meyer met directly with Navy Lieutenant Commander Charles Haffenden, who was in charge of the Naval Intelligence mission to make the port safe. A tentative agreement was reached — at least to the extent that Meyer agreed to talk to Charlie about helping the navy.

As a part of this development, Charlie was transferred from Dannemora to Great Meadows Prison, a much more comfortable environment. Meyer, Polakoff, and Costello traveled to Great Meadows to make the proposal to Charlie. Meyer outlined the navy's requests, suggesting compliance would be a service to the country, do Charlie no harm, and possibly even lead to a shortened sentence, early parole, or perhaps commutation. There had been no firm guarantees, but, when it was over, there would be considerable leverage at the least.

On their next visit, Charlie gave his answer: "I have no choice, let's do it." He had two stipulations: the assistance would be kept secret, and Meyer would be the sole intermediary to Charlie's people.

Meyer was given carte blanche to visit Charlie privately whenever he wished, as long as he was accompanied by Polakoff. One by one, Meyer took every relevant New York crime boss to Great Meadows to receive their initial instruction from Charlie, face-to-face. Within a month, the New York waterfront became the most secure port in the world.

Charles "Red" Haffenden was a career navy man who relished his role as spymaster. Despite his fascination with spy craft, he didn't always want to know the lengths to which the mobsters occasionally went to obtain results for him. While Meyer often had to work directly with Haffenden, he preferred to connect Haffenden to other people who could get the job done. One of these contacts was Johnny "Cockeye" Dunn, a power in the ILA. Dunn felt a personal obligation to the cause — Meyer and Haffenden had pulled strings to get him out of jail to work with them.

Dunn's enthusiasm sometimes took him a little over the top. Sniffing out spies and saboteurs became his forte. He would send men out as waiters, bartenders, and bellboys to eavesdrop. In one instance, two men who Haffenden believed were spies, but couldn't catch, simply disappeared.

Dunn admitted to nothing in regards to the disappearance, but he did offer that "they'll never bother us again."

Another maverick ILA man was John McCue. If work on the docks slowed down, McCue solved the problem, hurrying it along by breaking bones. This drew complaints from some of Haffenden's agents, who thought McCue was less than patient. Yet there was never a work stoppage, and the longshoremen were never more productive.

Charlie's instructions that all Italians in New York report anything suspicious to his people paid off one night when Meyer got a call from the brother of a panic-stricken fisherman. The fisherman had been fishing all night off Long Island when a U-boat had surfaced and landed four men on the beach. Meyer quickly passed the information to Haffenden, and the four — along with dynamite, armaments and sabotage plans — were captured.

Meyer acted as more than Charlie's middleman during the war years. He also arranged hospitality service jobs in the Dunn fashion for his "concerned citizens" of the anti-Bundist days. As well, he arranged to have Haffenden's agents service crime-controlled vending machines in bars and restaurants in order to conduct surveillance. Navy agents were also employed as Mob numbers runners to the same end.

At first they needed some job training, particularly in the fine points of the numbers racket. Even after the training, many seemed to ticket sellers rather odd choices to be trusted Mob collectors. First, most were young and clean-cut. They didn't speak Yiddish, Italian, or Sicilian; they spoke good English and none had New York accents. And, of all things, they were polite. Meyer was to say, "I think this must be the only time the U.S. Navy directly helped the mob." He reported that the money the agents turned over from their collections always tallied.

In 1942, the Allies successfully undertook a major offensive in North Africa. Now they turned their sights on Europe, more specifically the island of Sicily. This was Meyer's greatest challenge of the war.

Haffenden wanted every scrap of information obtainable about the island. That meant the who's who of every village, as well as the layouts of every village, road, bridge, and donkey track. How strong were the bridges? Which roads were impassable in rainstorms? And, naturally, who were the local mafiosi and Fascists? Haffenden wanted to know about fishing harbors, beaches, reefs, rocks, and tides up and down the coasts. Joe "Socks" Lanza managed to turn up a pair of elderly Sicilians, former fishermen, who knew more about the coasts than even a geographer could dream of.

Soon, Sicilians by the hundreds were being paraded into Haffenden's offices for interviews. Most brought with them letters, books, maps, and postcards from the Old Country. Of course, a few brought old vendettas, perhaps hoping the Allies would provide those named with "extra attention" during the chaos of the invasion. Only once did a New York Sicilian have to be taken to Great Meadows for an audience with Charlie before he would cooperate with Haffenden.

In July 1943, four of Haffenden's Sicilian-speaking agents landed on Sicily's beaches with the first U.S. Marines, then rapidly deployed inside German lines. They were armed with lists of local Unione Siciliane leaders, identified Allied sympathizers, and partisans. They carried letters from Sicilian émigrés. Along with these, they discovered that two names opened many doors when used in combination — Unione Siciliane and Charlie Luciano.

The four agents scored intelligence coup after coup: locations of minefields and booby traps and the routes to bypass them — and more to come. A local don, seeing a letter of authorization written to him by Charlie, led agents to a treasure trove that included the entire Axis troop dispositions in Sicily, current radio codes, and, reportedly, the disposition of Axis naval forces throughout southern Europe. The don, it happened, was an ex–New Yorker still wanted for murdering a New York policeman. Because the fugitive had been a teenager at the time of the murder, and as a favor to the man's family, Charlie had spirited him back to Sicily via Canada. Now he repaid a debt the agents didn't know existed.

Later, on the Italian mainland, local mafiosi led Haffenden's agents to a villa that housed Mussolini's personal archives, potentially of significant embarrassment to Hitler and other Axis leaders. The archives were a hot item, coveted by the Allies. They believed they would contain details of secret personal deals between Axis leaders, systematic looting and profiteering for personal gain, genocidal war crime evidence implicating Axis leaders, and dossiers of leaders' personal lives compiled by Mussolini for extortion purposes.

When Italy fell, Meyer and Charlie's role in the war effort was over, but there was still one detail to attend to — Charlie's prison sentence. Meyer and Polakoff continued to visit Charlie at Great Meadows, but meetings now likely had more to do with mutual interests rather than war news. For example, there was money to be made in counterfeit ration coupons and black market trade in many other goods. As well, gambling interests were still growing. Charlie and Meyer were of one mind sometimes — any opportunity to work a deal — and a small thing like imprisonment wasn't going to break down their rapport.

V.E. Day came and went, and still Charlie languished in Great Meadows. The U.S. Navy refused to acknowledge his support for the war effort, an essential admission if he was to obtain at least a sentence review. The navy's opposition to admitting to Charlie's support was so strong, Haffenden informed Meyer, that the balance of his own career would be jeopardized if he pursued the matter — this from a decorated war hero. The navy had taken the position that any hint it had relied on or consulted with mobsters would suggest its own weakness, leading to embarrassment and rumors that perhaps collusion went beyond a mutual war effort.

Meyer and Polakoff strenuously lobbied Governor Dewey for a commutation of Charlie's sentence. Finally, on

January 4, 1946, Dewey acquiesced, with the proviso that Charlie be immediately deported to Sicily. Rumors surfaced that Dewey had taken a large payoff in some form but these were never proved. They were so persistent, however, that in 1954, to clear the air, Dewey set up the Herlands Inquiry. It found no evidence against Dewey but did confirm Charlie and Meyer's contribution to the war effort. At the request of the U.S. Navy, the inquiry results were sealed until 1977.

Governor Dewey's reasons for the commutation were more likely partly humane and partly pragmatic. Dewey knew that Charlie's sentence was way out of line for the charges brought, especially given the dubious quality of evidence at his trial. He also knew that Charlie still controlled New York City's underworld from his cell. Instead of having him killed to get rid of him — not an option — he chose to have him deported. Perhaps if Charlie was stuck in Sicily, an ocean away, his power would wane.

After having served nearly 10 years in prison, Charlie "Lucky" Luciano was transferred to Sing Sing, then to Ellis Island. From there, he was placed aboard a less-than-luxurious ship, the *Laura Keene*, for the trip across the Atlantic. The boys decided to throw him a shipboard send-off party. The food was sumptuous, all Charlie's favorites. Joe Adonis rounded up several showgirls from the Copacabana to fill the dance cards. That night, as Charlie later reminisced in his autobiography, Pier 7 on the Brooklyn dock was barricaded by 200 burly longshoremen with baling hooks to ensure reporters got nowhere near the ship. Meyer probably attended the party but likely left early. In 1946, he was still performing his juggling act, perhaps more so than earlier.

During the war years, Cuba's gambling had been forced to shut down. With the war over, Meyer was anxious to get back to business as usual in Havana. When the Mob had secured Batista's cooperation in the 1930s they had moved quickly. Back then, through a New York bank Meyer had financed purchase of Havana's Ocean Park racetrack. Then he got on with establishing the Montmartre Casino, near Havana's best hotel, the Nacional. Both the racetrack and casino were immediately profitable, and Meyer then acquired the casino concession in the Nacional. All of Meyer's interests were in the capable hands of Lansky-schooled employees from the US, including brother Jake, working under Meyer's ever-watchful eye.

Meyer was also trying to work out deals to put casinos into Nassau and Freeport in the Bahamas. Complicating that matter, although only temporarily, his name had come up as the man who'd ordered a hit in 1943 on Sir Harry Oakes, a Canadian mining tycoon who lived in the Bahamas and was adamantly opposed to gambling being introduced. Sir Harry's death was never solved. The two Miami detectives investigating the case turned out to be less than competent, so much so that their fabricated evidence against Sir Harry's son-in-law was exposed.

Meyer was a traveling man again, still based in New

York, where it had all started for him, but still wanting to be on hand everywhere to scrutinize the daily take and the balance sheets.

Meyer also had two other balls in the air, one of which was Las Vegas, destined to become an American institution, and the other to become a personal torment.

Chapter 9
Family and Friends

Meyer may have come up aces when solving the problems of U.S. Navy Intelligence, but he might as well have been playing against a stacked deck when it came to solving those of his family. Ironically, he may have stacked the deck against himself without realizing it.

By 1940, Meyer's marriage to Anna existed in name only, and the pair of them usually shouted that sentiment at each other. Anna's feelings toward him were predominantly a mix of revulsion for Meyer's business and jealousy with respect to his frequent absences. When she could trace him, she would telephone him, often just to confirm he was where he was supposed to be and, with respect to hotels, that he was registered alone.

At home, they argued. Their son Buddy recalled occasions when arguments turned violent: Anna throwing things at Meyer, slamming him into walls, and, at least once, chasing him with a kitchen knife. Meyer also had a temper. He was not above slugging his wife or beating her in public.

Another powerful fear ate at Anna — that Meyer would bring Buddy and Paul into his business. This fear was unfounded. Meyer no more wanted his sons following in his footsteps than his own father had wanted Meyer in the garment trade. Still, Meyer did not send the boys to heder or insist they be bar mitzvahed. Instead, Buddy was placed in a special boarding school in Baltimore, and Paul was sent to West Point, a New York military academy. As soon as she was old enough, Meyer and Anna's daughter, Sandra, was enrolled in Fort Lauderdale's exclusive Pine Crest School, a private school from which she eventually graduated.

When the boys came home for Christmas in 1940, their mother was absent — in a special home, Meyer explained, "to get some rest." She would be in many more places like this throughout the rest of her life, sometimes being taken from the family's Central Park West apartment in a straitjacket.

Anna became increasingly delusional. She let her appearance go from haute couture to bag-lady shabby. In 1945, during a stay in a clinic, she received electroconvulsive therapy, which left her with fragmented memory, profound insecurity, and, overall, a worsened mental condition. According to Jake, Meyer had no patience for her and, in fact, continued browbeating her.

In late 1945, during a period of clarity, Anna filed for divorce. Proceedings took 16 months to work their way through the courts, but the decree was finally issued on Valentine's Day 1947. Meyer agreed to support payments and gave up custody of the three children with the exception that he held final authority over which schools and camps they attended. According to Doc Stacher, Meyer regularly provided Anna with more money than the stipulated payments.

As the marital legal maneuvering dragged through 1946, Meyer kept busy with various gambling enterprises. He found time that year to touch down in Los Angeles for a drive through the desert to Bugsy Siegel's "pink elephant" in Las Vegas — the Flamingo, then still under construction.

Bugsy had first gone to Las Vegas in 1941 to explore the possibility of establishing a horse racing wire service in the town. The State of Nevada had just legalized betting on wire-service race results. At the time, Las Vegas had one high-end resort complex, the El Rancho, a cross between a dude ranch and a casino. With new money pumped into the town by the war, a second resort, the Last Frontier, opened in 1942. It, too, leaned to the unsophisticated boots and spurs motif. Regardless, both were regularly overbooked. Bugsy decided he wanted in on the action, but his offers to buy both establishments were rejected.

Finally, in 1945, Bugsy had a chance to purchase a small hotel-casino named the El Cortez and persuaded Meyer to buy 10 percent. Meyer was somewhat skeptical about the Cortez's prospects and probably bought in just for old time's sake. As it turned out, Las Vegas real estate prices ballooned, and in July 1946, the Cortez was sold for an excellent profit.

Next Bugsy teamed up with a Californian, Ben Wilkerson, who had a dream of "bringing Beverly Hills and Sunset Strip to Las Vegas" — making it a true showplace in the desert. Wilkerson already owned land, had blueprints, and had started laying foundations for his enterprise. What he didn't have was enough money to finish the project. Enter Bugsy and his Cortez partners. They came on board Ben's project for a two-thirds interest and agreed that the new resort would be named the Flamingo. Again, Meyer bought in for 10 percent.

Bugsy was put in charge of wrapping up construction of the Flamingo. Then cost overruns for construction materials and furnishings went through the roof. With free rein, Bugsy, assisted and influenced by his mistress, Virginia Hill, insisted on the best of the best. The Flamingo was becoming a financial sinkhole, aggravated by Bugsy skimming money and hiding it in Switzerland.

Meyer had been aware of the cost overruns at the Flamingo site for some time, and certainly he knew about any skimming because he'd schooled Bugsy on how to use the Geneva and Zurich banks — two of them were run by Lansky Mob contacts. But Bugsy, the story goes, was so enamored of Virginia Hill, he couldn't think straight. He had already given up his wife and children for the infatuation.

Family and Friends

The Flamingo opened on December 26, 1946. Bugsy had met his own self-imposed deadline. On the stage that night were the immensely popular Xavier Cougat band, performer Jimmy Durante, and Baby Rose Marie, with George Jessel acting as master of ceremonies. George Raft, George Sanders, and Charles Coburn showed up in the audience, but the free charter flights Bugsy had arranged for many other Hollywood celebrities were grounded because of bad weather in Los Angeles.

Opening night was a bad one for the Flamingo Casino. The house lost heavily. To make matters worse, the guest rooms weren't ready, so Bugsy's guests decamped to other hotels where they could get a bed and, of course, gamble some more. Many did the latter. The Flamingo's competition did better that night than the Flamingo.

Meyer was not there for Bugsy's disastrous Christmas opening. He was having a Christmas party of his own that was far more important to him. And Meyer, the party planner, had done it up in style. For starters, he hadn't sent out invitations — he'd traveled the country to deliver them in person. The party was held at the Hotel Nacional in Havana. Along with the usual party favors the men of the Mob so cherished — food and drink, gambling and floor shows — Meyer booked a sure draw for his headliner: Frank Sinatra. An even more powerful draw was the party's true guest of honor — Charlie Luciano. Important business had to be discussed.

Charlie had arrived in Havana in late October via

Caracas and Mexico City. Meyer had offered to handle travel arrangements, but Charlie had turned him down, telling him he wouldn't have a problem from his end. Although Sicilian and Italian authorities were keeping their eyes on Charlie, since he hadn't broken any of their laws (that they knew of), he was granted a passport as Salvatore Lucania, as well as visas to Mexico, Cuba, and Venezuela. He cruised through customs like visiting royalty and was installed in an upscale villa arranged by Meyer. The Cuban Minister of the Interior provided Charlie a permit to stay in Cuba as long as he wanted.

Charlie presided over the weeklong business meeting. His agenda was the future, and the major thrust of that would be gambling on a world-class scale. The plan was put forward to turn Cuba's Isle of Pines — today the site of Fidel Castro's most infamous prison — into a complex that would rival Monte Carlo. Bugsy's plan for Las Vegas paled by comparison. Charlie also exacted allegiances at the Havana meeting and, as could be expected, all present endorsed his plans.

There was some minor opposition. Doc Stacher put it another way: "A number of the younger guys were doubtful about paying allegiance to the old-timer, as they called him, but Meyer backed him 100 percent and nobody wanted to cross the Little Man. He was handling most of their finances and was the key figure in the gambling income. Meyer kept in the background as always, but nobody at that meeting had the faintest doubt who held the whip hand."

To this point, the meeting had been upbeat. Discussions had focused on successes and future opportunities. But there was a final piece of business to discuss. Meyer had to report on an investment that appeared to be going sour, the Flamingo.

Having persuaded many Mob figures to invest in the Flamingo, Meyer was obliged to tell them that forecast costs for construction and initial operating capital might hit $6 million. This was a far cry from the $1.2 million originally estimated. In short, the project would need more money. While he probably didn't tell them Bugsy had been turned down for another loan from a legitimate bank, he was obliged to inform investors that it appeared Bugsy and Virginia had secreted as much as half a million dollars, money skimmed from the investments, to a Swiss bank account.

As Meyer knew, the men he was addressing were not the average shareholders. Their practices didn't include waiting for the next annual meeting to voice concerns, going to a securities commission to file a complaint, or hiring a battery of lawyers to pummel Bugsy with lawsuits. Meyer pleaded with the assembly to give his friend a little more time. Even as they were enjoying Christmas in Havana, Bugsy was officially opening the Flamingo in Las Vegas. "Let's wait and see," he entreated. Somberly, Meyer was asked to leave the room while the issue was discussed.

Meyer had done his best for his friend, but over the years he'd learned that, when friendship and business mix, business remains primary. There had been times when he had ordered it so himself. To have been asked to leave the room showed consideration for his friendship with Bugsy, and certainly respect for Meyer, but now business had to be divorced from friendship.

According to Doc Stacher, just before Sinatra took the stage at the Christmas party, Charlie took Meyer aside. "Meyer," he said, "I know your feelings for Bugsy ... but Meyer, this is business and Bugsy has broken our rules. He is betraying us. He is cheating us. He knows it and you know it."

Charlie added, "Unless Bugsy makes a great success of that hotel, you know as well as I do that he'll have to be shot. And if you don't have the heart to do it, Meyer, I will have to order the execution myself."

On December 27, the holidayers at the Hotel Nacional heard about Bugsy's opening night fiasco. Meyer went to bat for him again, stressing the long-term payoff of the Flamingo. His reputation, built over decades of straight dealing, was on the line. But Charlie backed him, and together the pair got Bugsy more money and a bit more time.

Bugsy then used the time to marry Virginia in Mexico and ship her off to Europe. He was forced to close the Flamingo at the end of January, but in March he re-opened it. The Andrews Sisters headlined. With Virginia far away, Bugsy seemed, finally, to be taking care of business. The Flamingo began to show a profit. In May, he reported a quarter million dollar profit to investors. By mid-June, he apparently felt he could breathe easier.

Not so. On the evening of June 20, 1947, Bugsy was sitting on a couch in Virginia Hill's home reading the *Los Angeles Times*. The first bullet from a .30 caliber army carbine shattered a vertebra in his neck, mashed his right eye, and crushed the bridge of his nose. The next sent his other eyeball 15 feet across the room, but that second bullet, and the seven more that followed, didn't matter much. The first had been sufficient.

The news hit radio stations within an hour. By then, in Las Vegas, Moe Sedway and Gus Greenbaum, two partners in the casino, were tidying house at the Flamingo. "We are now under new management," they announced. No one argued. Greenbaum, together with other hands-on investors, clearly demonstrated they were in charge. Every one of them was an experienced professional gambling man, schooled in Meyer's gambling operations for years. As for Meyer, he still held his 10 percent. Within a year, the Las Vegas situation was not only stabilized, but blossoming. The Flamingo went on to become a huge moneymaker.

While the Flamingo turned the corner to profitability, Bugsy's murder remained unsolved. Notwithstanding the profits he'd reported in May, Bugsy's cardinal sin of skimming from investors had remained an unforgivable act. Charlie had given him a chance to make the Flamingo a moneymaker, and he'd risen to the opportunity. Despite that, in no recounting of Charlie's conversations with Meyer did Charlie ever say he would forgive the skimming.

Meyer did not authorize the murder. Nor did he go out of his way to prevent it, though he probably couldn't have if he'd wanted to. Indeed, it did not surprise him. He knew his people — Sedway and Greenbaum had worked with Meyer on the Lower East Side since before the early Saratoga Springs days — and he knew their harsh style of doing business. There were other investors who held to the same business methods and ethics. He was one of them. Doubtless, Bugsy's murder had been approved by the Commission. Had it not, either Charlie or Meyer would have exacted quick and deadly vengeance in some form, and there is no indication such occurred in the months that followed.

Beyond his efforts on Bugsy's behalf at the Havana meetings and then arranging for the bridge financing Bugsy required to complete construction, Meyer's direct involvement in Las Vegas matters appeared negligible during 1947. By then, Meyer had relocated to Hollywood, Florida, to be close to his clubs there. Jake had also relocated, and his was the name on the ownership papers for Meyer's spectacular Colonial Inn in Hallandale. In addition, Meyer was traveling regularly to Havana to oversee his gambling holdings and re-establish a sugar cane concession he'd obtained from Batista for Molaska Corporation. The latter was still heavily involved in distilling liquor for the bootleg market, which continued to thrive.

For at least six months of each year, Meyer lived modestly in a rented house on a beach in Hollywood. His newspaper, milk, and bread were delivered daily to his door. He didn't holler at neighborhood kids if their baseballs rolled onto his lawn, and he gave out candy at Halloween. Records show that he was also a member of the Book-of-the-Month Club. Meyer was being invisible.

Periodically, he traveled to New York to visit Buddy, but he eventually moved Buddy down to Florida, putting him in charge of running a small motel on the fringe of the Florida Keys. While in New York, he also looked after business. Then he would spend much of July and August tending to the needs of the racing crowd of the still-thriving Saratoga Springs.

In late August 1948, shortly after his return to Hollywood from Saratoga Springs, feeling refreshed and ready for the influx of snowbirds, Meyer met his next-door neighbor, Thelma "Teddy" Schwartz. While heading out to get some dinner one evening, he bumped into her and her girlfriend. Ever the gentleman, Meyer invited them to join him.

Teddy "kind of" knew his business, but to her, it was *his* business — none of her concern, not ever. When they met, she was nearly divorced after 20 years of marriage and had one son, facts that were of no consequence to Meyer. Four months after he met her, just days after her divorce was finalized, Meyer married her.

It may have been love, plain and simple, but maybe one of the attractions for Meyer was that Teddy was three inches shorter than him— not many people in his circle were shorter than Meyer Lansky. She was fiercely dedicated to her new husband, outspoken sometimes to the point of rudeness (once spitting on an aggressive reporter at the Miami airport), and, for Meyer, probably a delightful relief after the years of stress he had endured with Anna. Meyer's sister, Esther, called Teddy "his liberation." Other relatives thought she was a loud-mouthed pest.

Also in 1948, Meyer began to show an interest in Israel. He was approached to run a charity auction at the Colonial Inn — a pedestrian matter, since he did so regularly to bolster his image as a community booster and humanitarian. This one, however, was on behalf of Haganah, one of several militant organizations working for the autonomy of an Israeli state in the Middle East. The auction was a success, raising $10,000. Soon after, Haganah representatives approached him with quite a different request, one that involved no pictures in the local press, no civic presentation as citizen of the month, and not a scrap of positive publicity for the Colonial.

Haganah asked Meyer to use his connections to disrupt arms shipments from a Pittsburgh arms dealer to Palestinian nationalists. The new state of Israel was fighting for its existence against the combined assault of the Middle East Arab states and the British government, all of whom were supporting the Palestinians.

Meyer traveled to New York immediately, where he spoke with some of his contacts on the docks, people who'd worked with him gathering intelligence and had ensured the safe passage of men and munitions during the war years.

Soon, Palestinian arms shipments out of New York began falling into Israeli hands — no pirating on the high seas or any such derring-do, just changes of ships and bills of lading. Crates of machine guns and mortars, cargo holds of bullets, shells, and grenades would be loaded on a ship bound for Tel Aviv rather than Tripoli or Cairo. "I guess the paperwork got screwed up," Meyer said many times with a shrug. "Hell, New York's a busy harbor, mistakes happen."

Other loads were simply dumped in the harbor, and a few were destroyed in warehouse fires. Meyer's contacts persuaded the Pittsburgh dealer and others to inform them whenever the Palestinians made a purchase. With contacts up and down the East Coast waterfronts, Meyer made it impossible for shipments to move without his knowledge.

Meyer went as far as helping the Haganah establish its intelligence and arms purchasing offices on the second floor of Frank Costello's Copacabana Club. Moreover, as he had done for U.S. Naval Intelligence, he put Haganah agents in direct contact with his resources on the docks.

Meyer threw himself into providing support to the Haganah. The cause of Israel became his cause. No doubt he cashed in a lot of favors to help them; remarkable for him given he obtained no profit, except, perhaps, spiritually and emotionally, by remembering his grandfather's dreams. His grandfather had dreamed of Zion, a Promised Land for Jews. His father's dream had proved to be less than golden; perhaps his grandfather's would be realized.

Meyer Lansky

Meyer was now moving into middle age and had been involved in criminal activity for most of his teenage and adult life. Yet he seemed unscathed by the law. In the early 1950s, he received only passing mention in the final report of Senator Estes Kefauver's Special Committee to Investigate Organized Crime in Interstate Commerce. When Kefauver met Meyer, Meyer appeared simply to be a little man who happened to have interests in gambling. Kefauver had a weakness for gambling himself. Meyer, who always did his homework, knew this. Doubtless, he managed to convey this knowledge and with that may have somewhat whittled Kefauver's sword of justice.

Middle-aged, a new wife, successful on most fronts — presumably Meyer could slow down, put a few balls he was juggling back on the shelf. He was not a made man in the Mafia sense; he wasn't locked into the rackets for life. Or was he?

Chapter 10
The Might
of Government

After World War II, Meyer had some difficulty re-establishing himself in Havana. The Cold War was nearly hot and tourism from the United States to Cuba was being discouraged. The U.S. State Department pressured him to suggest to Cuba's ostensibly pro-Communist dictator, Batista, that he resign. Already, by threatening an embargo on U.S. medical supply exports to the country, the U.S. government had compelled Batista to forcibly expel Charlie in April of 1947. To the extent Batista was losing his influence, so, too, was Meyer.

Batista resigned in 1948, proclaimed a democratic election to satisfy the demands of the United States, then, in a typical banana republic–style election, arranged that a stooge be elected. That cooled the political heat for a time.

In 1952, however, Batista decided he wanted his spotlight back, staged a quick coup, and once again declared himself president. At about the same time he moved back into his presidential palace, the *Saturday Evening Post* reported that gambling in Havana was so corrupt only one casino was operating honestly — the Montmartre Club, which, not surprisingly, was Meyer's.

To counter the bad press, Batista hired the only honest casino operator in Havana as his "adviser on gambling reform." That man was Meyer. In quick time, Meyer cleaned house. Cardsharps were deported en masse. Several casino operators decided it was timely to sell out and depart the island, while others quickly cleaned up their act. New security measures were introduced to ensure honesty at the tables. Meyer had had to do the same in Havana for free in the 1930s; now he was doing it on retainer.

In 1955, a subsidiary of Pan American Airlines took over Meyer's coveted Hotel Nacional but leased him space for a bar and restaurant, a showroom for entertainment, and, most important, a casino. This was all well and good, but Meyer had bigger plans — so big he was prepared to sell his interest in the Nacional as soon as he opened his new showcase. He called it the Havana Riviera. The Riviera had 440 double rooms, central air conditioning (a Havana first), and 21 stories. But the centerpiece of the Riviera was its casino — there was none finer in the world.

Meyer's new hotel opened on December 10, 1957. All of

the rooms were pre-booked for the winter of 1957–58, thanks partly to the marketing skills of Ben and Harry Smith, experienced Toronto hoteliers whom Meyer had contracted as overall managing directors of the Riviera Hotel Corporation, the holding company.

On the books, Meyer was listed as the Riviera's kitchen director, at an IRS-declared salary of $36,500 annually. Curiously, Meyer did supervise every detail of the Riviera's kitchens, almost taking more pride in this accomplishment than in the casino floor itself. Any VIP he took on a tour always saw the kitchens first.

Seats in the showroom, the Copa, were scalped for hundreds of dollars apiece. The opening show, starring Ginger Rogers, made it to American network television. But Meyer was reportedly disappointed with her performance. "She can wiggle her ass," he supposedly said, "but she can't sing a goddamn note." No one else seemed to care; they were all eyes and having a splendid time.

Through the Havana Riviera, Meyer demonstrated his prowess as a casino operator. Meanwhile, his people were busy demonstrating their own prowess in Las Vegas. Having turned the Flamingo around, they added other hotel-casinos to their empire: the Sands, managed by Doc Stacher; the Thunderbird; the Riviera; and coming up fast, the Desert Inn. All were financed through the convoluted money channels Meyer had masterminded.

In December 1958, the Havana Riviera was gearing up

for its second major season. But by January 1959, none of these plans and preparations mattered. Fidel Castro came to power. The casinos were shut down. Meyer, beset with severe ulcer attacks, struggled through negotiations with Castro's government. Briefly, the casinos reopened, but they were losing money. On October 24, 1960, Castro finally dropped the ax and nationalized US-owned holdings in Cuba. The Havana Riviera was one of these. No compensation was offered.

Meyer Lansky, 58 years old, was a sick man, physically and financially. He had invested millions of his own money in the Havana Riviera, and it was a write-off. His ulcer problems were compounded by a heart condition, made all the worse by a whole other set of problems brewing in Nevada.

Las Vegas development boomed in the 1950s, and Meyer owned points in many of its casinos. Besides instituting honest games on the casino floors, Meyer had orchestrated the mechanics of the skim, which passed hundreds of millions of dollars into mob pockets. In some Vegas casinos, as much as 20 percent of the daily gross was skimmed before the cash went into counting rooms, where the Nevada Gaming Commission could monitor it.

But, by the 1960s, the Mob was forcing Jewish interests out of Las Vegas, a process that had started as early as 1953. It was as if they had forgotten who had put them in the city to begin with and demonstrated the subtleties of squeezing money from the desert oasis. Mobsters became too omnipresent, too ostentatious, and too aggressive — in a word, stupid.

Meyer sold out any holdings he had and left the Mob to wallow in its excesses. They didn't do it for long. The Gaming Commission and Department of Justice tired of them and, soon, they too found themselves on the outside looking in.

Meyer, meanwhile, still had an arrow in his quiver: the Bahamas. By 1961, casino projects were rapidly moving forward on the islands, notably in New Providence, where a company with the unlikely name of Mary Carter Paints — later renamed Resorts International — was building a hotel-casino complex on Paradise Island. Later disclosures indicated that gambling licenses had been obtained with payoffs to government officials — no surprise. An exposé in the *Wall Street Journal* also alleged that Meyer was the spearhead for the Resorts International development — again, no surprise.

The real surprise came when the name of one of the major shareholders in Mary Carter Paints was revealed — none other than Thomas E. Dewey. Interestingly, Dewey did not divest himself of his stock when the company renamed itself, or even when the *Journal* pounced on his involvement. Old questions arose when the *Journal* published the article. Why did Dewey commute Charlie's sentence back in 1946 when the U.S. Navy was adamantly opposed to doing so? Was there truth to the persistent rumor that the Mob contributed cash to Dewey's presidential bid so that, if he won, he would pave the way to Charlie's re-entering the United States? Did Dewey ever catch a major crime figure who wasn't handed to him by the mob? Was Louis Buchalter's conviction based on knowingly perjured testimony, and didn't J. Edgar Hoover and Walter Winchell actually make the bust after Lepke had laughed at and outrun Dewey for two years?

While there were countless questions and allegations surrounding Dewey's link to mobsters and his investment in Resorts International, the Lansky tie-in to Paradise Island was generally indisputable, linked through two associates: Eddie Collini, who managed the Paradise Island operation, and his brother Dino, who was involved with the Lucayan Beach Casino in Freeport, Grand Bahama Island. The brothers had long worked in Meyer's gambling operations, including those in Havana. However, the allegations brought forth by the *Journal* that Meyer spearheaded Resorts International were never proven.

The Bahamas in the 1960s were ideal for the Lansky operational style in two major respects. There was the prerequisite of corruptible government officials. Second, and more ideal, banking in the Bahamas was as secretive as in Switzerland. The skim didn't need to be flown halfway across the world before it could be put back into circulation. It could be walked across the street and put in the night deposit box.

With a change of government in 1967, however, the roof came down on the mobsters, though not to the same extent as in Cuba. In the islands, they were allowed to sell their holdings. Resorts International went to Donald Trump, and then to Merv Griffin.

The Might of Government

By then, Meyer had moved on. Publicity was hurting him terribly. The myth of Meyer as the Machiavelli of the Mob was being built in the American media. Indeed, by that point, the media had no one else left from the era of the gangsters — Dutch Schultz and Louis Buchalter were long dead; Al Capone, the scourge of Chicago, had bitten it; and even Charlie was gone — he had died of an unexpected heart attack at the Naples airport on January 26, 1962. Charlie had had a long-standing history of heart ailments.

So the media turned to Meyer, inventing their own mastermind, the Little Man. Aiming to satisfy the American public's love/hate fascination with organized crime, writers provided their readers with story after story on Meyer Lansky, a real-life crime figure. With all the attention, the U.S. government felt compelled to act. From the late 1960s until Meyer died, government from the highest national level made every effort to make his life miserable. Perhaps the most vindictive thing the government did was stifle his attempt to become an Israeli citizen and live out his last days in Israel.

Meyer had first traveled to Israel in 1962 as part of a holiday with Teddy. He was impressed enough to return in 1970, when he sought out the graves of his grandparents, Benjamin and Basha. In many respects, Meyer, now an old man far distanced in influence and interests in the rackets, was nostalgically looking for his roots, a personal, if tenuous, tie to when his life seemed far less complicated and far more idealistic. At the age of 69, in December of 1970, he applied for Israeli citizenship.

The US government, however, decided it wasn't finished with Meyer. In the 1950s, authorities had tried to have him deported because of his false declaration on his naturalization papers — that he had no criminal record. Of course, the Immigration and Naturalization Department's case never made it to court. Records had been misplaced or destroyed, and possible witnesses had either died, forgotten circumstances, or were simply not credible enough to withstand cross-examination by the powerhouse lawyers Meyer could be expected to have at his defense table.

Ironically, in 1971, the government was doing what it could to bring Meyer back from Israel to the United States. Officials demanded his presence to appear before a grand jury investigating potential indictments for tax evasion and contempt in Miami. Meanwhile, legal battles were already raging over his bid for Israeli citizenship. Unfortunately for Meyer, Israeli and international media, preferring myth to meat, pilloried him. Rumors flew in the Israeli press, including one alleging that Meyer was fronting an organized crime attempt to buy up Tel Aviv tourist hotels.

The Israeli prosecution sought to prove that Meyer would be a criminal influence if granted citizenship. In an effort to help the prosecution's case, the U.S. government supplied the Israelis with every scrap of information federal agencies had gathered on Meyer throughout his lifetime.

These included his tax returns, criminal record (mostly gambling offenses), suspicious or perjured testimony and affidavits, illegal wiretaps, the criminal records of associates, and anything else the Department of Justice thought might stymie his application.

Meyer's lawyer presented his case directly to Prime Minister Golda Meier, herself a Lower East Side resident in her childhood. Those roots didn't help his cause; she loathed any reference to the Mob, knowing its corrupting power. At the time, Prime Minister Meier was striving to obtain Phantom F4 fighter planes from Richard Nixon's administration. Some say she made a straight trade: Meyer for the fighters. More likely, she traded him for American public opinion, which not only smoothed the way for the fighters but ensured continuing American support for other Israeli needs. Meyer's ultimate deportation back to the States was an expedient move by Israeli courts.

In November 1972, Meyer ended up in Miami. He was arrested for contempt of court, posted bail of $250,000, and went directly to a hospital. Meyer's heart condition had been severely exacerbated by the stressful, drawn-out fight in Israeli courts. He was 71 years old, and a very tired man.

Meyer eventually recovered his health sufficiently to attend court. The trial was brief, and he was acquitted. The government charges may have had some legitimacy — he'd failed to show up and honor a grand jury subpoena — but at bottom they were bogus. In the last court judgment on record, in response to the prosecutor's filing of a leave to appeal, the presiding judge wrote that he "did not think Lansky's importance is justification for a petition for a proposed writ of certiorari. On the contrary, the filing of such a virtually frivolous petition would be an open act of intellectual dishonesty."

In any case, John Mitchell's Department of Justice was occupied at that time with extricating itself from the Watergate scandal and had no time for a man near the end of his mortal coil.

Although he now lived in Miami most of the year, Meyer still had ties in New York City. Sandra, his daughter, lived there. Anna, his first wife, lived out her days there. Meyer visited periodically, mostly to socialize with old pals from the East Side. In Miami, Meyer and Teddy lived modestly. He walked his dog daily and read the *Miami Herald* while eating breakfast at a local café. Teddy did the grocery shopping at neighborhood supermarkets. Occasionally the couple would cab it to a family restaurant for dinner. If someone knocked at their door, Teddy would answer, still fiercely protective of her man. Wherever Meyer went, government agents doggedly tailed him, perhaps still hoping to turn his myth into reality.

Meyer Lansky died of heart failure, in his bed, on January 15, 1983. He was survived by Teddy, his two sons and daughter, and Jake. Buddy remained under care for the rest of his life, helped out over the years by Meyer's old friend, Jimmy Blue Eyes, who was also the nominal executor of Meyer's estate. Probate showed property in New York City, his home in Miami, a few bucks in the bank, and some stock in a natural gas exploration company — nothing near the $300 million media and government alleged he'd stashed over the years. However, since Meyer presumably used Swiss or Bahamian bank accounts and never put anything important on paper, it's possible he carried the account numbers and passwords only in his head, taking them to his grave.

Epilogue

Definitely, Meyer Lansky, a man with a lifelong fascination for gambling, carried the memory of a major piece of American culture to his grave. He was in the room when many of the major decisions that shaped organized crime in the United States were made, from structure to administration to tactics.

He was a mover, but only when faced with no other options was he a shaker. His myth, if not his practices, put big-time high-gross gambling on the American map, from slot machines, punch cards, and "policy," to the click of dice and the whirl and plop of the roulette ball.

Meyer lived the part of history that experienced the maturation of American gambling: from street crap games into the back rooms of saloons, speakeasies, and sleazy nightclubs, then to lake houses and carpet joints, and, finally, to lavish casinos. Meyer didn't do it all, but he was there, a mythical magic man who made the "house" the ruler of the gambling universe. It still is.

About the Author

Ottawa-based Art Montague writes fiction as well as non-fiction, but his interests in history, biography, and crime remain constant. He is a member of Crime Writers of Canada and the Periodical Writers Association of Canada.

Photo Credits

Cover: AP/Wide World Photo; Library of Congress: page 41.

Further Reading

Balsamo, William, and George Carpozi Jr. *Under the Clock: The Inside Story of the Mafia's First 100 Years.* Far Hills, N.J.: New Horizon Press, 1988.

Cohen, Rich. *Tough Jews: Fathers, Sons, and Gangster Dreams.* New York: Simon & Schuster, 1998.

Eisenberg, Dennis, Uri Dan, and Eli Landau. *Meyer Lansky: Mogul of the Mob.* New York: Paddington Press, 1979.

Lacey, Robert. *Little Man: Meyer Lansky and the Gangster Life.* Boston: Little, Brown & Company, 1991.

Messick, Hank. *Lansky.* London: Robert Hale & Company, 1973.

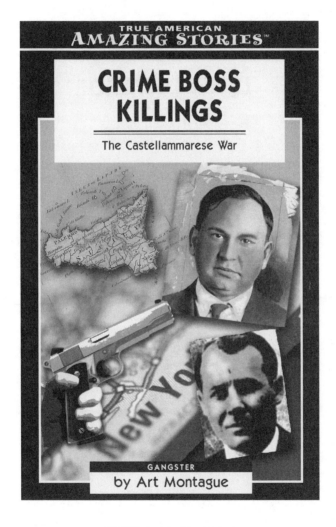

TRUE AMERICAN
AMAZING STORIES™

CRIME BOSS KILLINGS

The Castellammarese War

GANGSTER

by Art Montague

ISBN 1-55265-101-0